WOODLAND WALKS
in South-West England

Webb & Bower

O|S Ordnance Survey

WOODLAND WALKS
in South-West England
Gerald Wilkinson

First published in Great Britain in 1986 by
Webb & Bower (Publishers) Limited,
9 Colleton Crescent, Exeter, Devon EX2 4BY, and
Ordnance Survey,
Romsey Road, Maybush, Southampton S09 4 DH
in association with
Michael Joseph Limited,
27 Wright's Lane,London W8 5SL

Designed by Peter Wrigley

Production by Nick Facer

British Library Cataloguing in Publication Data

Wilkinson, Gerald
   The Ordnance Survey woodland walks in
   South-West England.
   1. Forests and forestry—England
   2. Walking—England
   I. Title
   914.23′04858   SD179
   ISBN 0–86350–054–4

Typeset in Great Britain by Keyspools Limited, Golborne, Lancashire
Printed and bound in Great Britain by Hazell Watson and Viney Limited,
Member of the BPCC Group, Aylesbury, Bucks

TITLE PAGE
Ashes and other trees on the ramparts of an
Iron Age fort at Chastleton, near Chipping
Norton in the Cotswolds. See page 92.

Contents

Introduction

The south-western quarter of England, containing our greatest forests, our oldest enclosed land, many prehistoric settlements, the National Arboretum (and our finest coastline), hardly needs an introduction. This volume covers the whole of the West Country, and takes in Wiltshire, Gloucestershire and Herefordshire.

Withy, oak, elm and ash: these Cornish trees were planted by St Keyne at her well (south of Liskeard), one of many in Cornwall with magic properties. It is said that when a storm blew down the trees, which had formed an arch, the waters lost their properties. These were rather strange: whoever of a newly wed pair first drank the water would be master of the household. The same power is conferred on those who sit in St Michael's chair, on the tower of the church of St Michael's Mount. Most of Cornwall's magic comes from mineral rather than vegetable sources, and large areas of the county are barren of trees, but, ironically, almost any trees, including subtropical palms, will grow in the sheltered, frost-free coves. No one has cared for the Cornish woods, except for a few landowners on the south coast, where there are one or two scraps of woodland nature reserves. One lovely cove in which the Cornish elm had formed a wood is now full of the dead trees; maybe they will grow again from root sucker shoots – suckers are the elm's usual way of reproducing. The moorlands, too far away from England to have a history of Forest Law, have been grazed since prehistoric times, until the Forestry Commission began reafforestation (after a gap of 4000 years) at Halvana on Bodmin Moor and in an experimental patch on Goonhilly Downs. The long-term improvement to these dreary wastes by the growing of spruce trees will not be great, but the side effects – drainage, fences, shelter – encourage the return of native plants and birds.

It's the coastline that counts, of course. On the part of it that I know well, you need blinkers to appreciate it. But perhaps it is not typical. Inland, between Newquay and Padstow, are many little dells full of miniature woodland of a peculiar richness and sweetness which ought to be made into nature reserves before some enterprising persons install mobile (ie stationary) homes.

To me, the Devonshire countryside is perfect; richly coloured and well formed in every detail, with familiar trees more beautifully shaped than anywhere else. Devon has, they say, as many miles of road as the whole of Belgium, most of which are wandering, intricate lanes that seem to go nowhere. It is the oldest enclosed countryside in Britain, and a single parish may have, on average, as many as 160 miles of hedges. Hedges are not strips of woodland – they more resemble scrubland – but they are the nearest thing to woodland in most of lowland Devonshire. Seventy-five per cent of the hedges in Devon have in them between four to eight different species, which means, according to the famous Cooper count, that they date from between 1200 and 1600: an astonishing antiquity; and a small percentage are older, with nine or ten species. Added to this, the banks on which they grow may be a century older still. Few English counties can boast hedges going back before Domesday.

Like a separate country, Dartmoor also has its mysteries and antiquities, in our case enshrined in three tiny woods. Between the moorland edges and the farmlands, and in the lower valleys of the Dartmoor streams, are woodlands lovely enough and in quantity sufficient to make Devon famous for no other reason. The two Forestry Commission plantations, Fernworthy and Bellever, keep fairly low profiles and are very well shaped. Fernworthy particularly has wonderful approaches behind Chagford and encloses a beautiful marsh full of sallows. A stone circle under dark spruces gains in mysteriousness and looks somehow exactly right in its environment of American trees.

North Devon, apart from Exmoor, has fine coastal woods and some rather wild, heathy forests – I found Hartland fascinating.

The beech hedges on the eastern and southern slopes of Exmoor are impressive, and reassuring to anyone who thought the art of hedging is lost. 'While Dunkery frowns on Exon Moor' for Hardy, Minehead has flourishing cabbage palms (*Cordyline*) and fern palms (*Chamaetops*) for softer souls; and more forestry from Croydon Hill to the Vale of Taunton. The Forestry Commission has raped the Brendon Hills, and they will never recover, even with the corners preserved by the National Trust. But, typically, the Commission has provided access, where there might have been none, and a fine viewpoint approached by a wheelchair track from a group of fine old beeches.

The wetlands of Sedgemoor are by all accounts a lost cause, though the roadsides often retain their beauty, and the prehistoric tradeways of coppice poles, discovered here, are worth exploring.

Down south, in the eastern corner of Devon, are some touching traces of old forests at Ashclyst and Neroche. On the coast, near the Dorset border, is a nature reserve, the Lyme Regis landslip, that should not be missed.

Dorset more or less defeated me – I suppose I am not the first. Seeking out the forested areas I tended to miss the downs and heaths where native woodland waits to be discovered. Even so, as long as you repair one of my omissions and go to Tollard Royal, you will not find this chapter a bad guide. As for heathland, the New Forest casts its shadow before it; perhaps it should not be allowed to influence an approach to Purbeck, with its many nature reserves. Powerstock Common, a nature reserve to the west, is remarkable for a great variety of habitat, including a well looked-after oakwood and a poetic piece of old railway.

My fifty-kilometre squares deal divisively with the borders of Hampshire and Wiltshire. The ideal would have been to create ecological divisions, but this could lead to false boundaries and, what one should never do to Britain, over-simplifying. Section 7 does at least isolate the New Forest, the most important woodland area in the whole country. The land now largely occupied by Southampton and Bournemouth, the Hampshire Basin, was the cradle of the British forest. The last ice of the Ice Ages passed it by, and the trees now native to Wales and Scotland, and perhaps some others, survived there until they were joined by the advancing army of more warmth-demanding trees from Europe. The New Forest itself, on higher, badly drained ground, remains a key to all the history of our landscape with its pattern of ancient woodland and at least as ancient rights of common, particularly grazing rights. A considerable book would be needed to guide one through all its walks.

At Grovely Wood, north-west of Salisbury, above W. H. Hudson's favourite Wylye, you can see how ancient woodland can be transformed into a softwood factory. The destruction started not with the Forestry Commission but through the siting of an airfield runway.

Up in the north-east corner of the section, Harewood Forest is much more traditional, in spite of a wartime phase of concrete laying, and can show a convincingly mediaeval-looking coppice with the smoke of charcoal burning drifting through. This is a private not a state forest.

The simple triangulation of the Isle of Wight does not constitute a survey, but may form a useful introduction to a very intriguing place.

Westonbirt appears to be actually in Gloucestershire, but it lies in the north Wiltshire clay, near Tetbury and Malmesbury. The National Arboretum at Westonbirt is certainly the most attractive place in Britain for lovers of trees; but do not expect to get to know Westonbirt in one visit. As a place to research almost any tree that will grow in Britain, it is unsurpassed. Perhaps it lacks the rigour and 'architectural' quality of Bedgebury's rolling avenues, for it is flat, and sometimes it seems rather a jumble, with fir groves or stands of single species. But it really is a heavenly place at any season.

The Mendips are rich in woodland and very much tourist country. Leigh Woods, near

Bristol, are important for their local *Sorbus* species and also because they are so near to a great city. Weston Woods and Cleeve are worth exploring.

If you imagine that the Swindon area has little woodland, you are right. The Downs are close, however, and you can climb out of this western slough to Calne for a nice arboretum or to the great Savernake Forest. Here the beeches are so tall that it is a matter of urgency to see them before the foresters decide they are too good to stay. Of all the forests, Savernake is the most approachable and the most rewarding in terms of pure woodland. Many ancient trees, including oaks and thorns, are preserved. The Forestry Commission, perhaps feeling that a forest should be full of roasting meat, provides barbecue hearths, but you have to bring your own venison.

The Wiltshire Downs I always thought of as somewhat feminine compared with the more forthright-sounding Berkshire Downs. Not so; there is nothing 'wilting' about them. The Downs and the downland villages get progressively more twee as you travel towards Highclere, where much of the woodland is either strictly private or dreary.

I tried, and failed, to make a woodland walk in willows, alders and poplars along the Kennet and Avon Canal, getting very muddy in the process. It is still a good canal walk, if you take your wellies, west from Newbury. There are some very good woods in a ring around the north of Newbury – some of these have escaped into our south-east volume. South of Greenham Common, towards Watership Down, is a narrow road with no overtones and a lot of footpaths to be explored. Beyond the motorway (take the pleasant

B4000) northwards to Oxfordshire, the Lambourn Downs are fascinating and not without woods. I have been unable to find a decent wood to walk in, in the Vale of the White Horse, at least west of Abingdon. I can recommend the lanes about Kelmscott, Filkin and Langford – almost my home countryside.

The great Forest of Dean is almost equal in importance to the New Forest and the Dartmoor National Park, and a lot more could be said about it than can be said here. With the Wye Valley included there is a potential book-length survey here. However, the Dean Forest is not perfect. The Forestry Commission, at least nowadays, cannot be accused of destructiveness. Their brief is first to produce softwood, second to provide access. They are doing these things, and more. But the Forest of Dean is like a rather intricate egg from which the foresters have ever so carefully sucked the contents and replaced them with something else. The shell remains intact, and it is a very diversely patterned and beautiful shell. Not to pursue the rather difficult simile, traditions also are maintained and in no empty form. The numbers of Freeminers in the forest may even grow, who knows.

The Wye Valley remains to be mentioned. Well, plenty of native woods remain, and are quiet, while the Gorge buzzes with tourists. Symonds Yat you would think was Niagara from the numbers that come to stare. And Tintern, so inspiring to the picturesque and romantic press and watercolourists, can still be splendidly portrayed by modern photographers. The best walks in the Wye Valley are around Blackcliff and Wyndcliff, technically in Gwent, a couple of nature reserves and National Trust land.

Key

The book is divided into sections which follow on numerically from west to east and south to north of the region. At the beginning of each section the relevant Ordnance Survey Landranger sheet numbers are listed. Each entry is headed with factual information in the form below:

         a   **b**   **c**

Burrator Forest *568 694*, ♀ ✿, *1000 acres, paths and a forest road, WA*

       d   **e**

a Ordnance Survey National Grid reference – usually of the nearest car park
b Type of woodland: ♀ deciduous
                       ✦ coniferous ✿ marsh
c Size of wooded area
d Type of walk
e Owner of site

How to find a grid reference

The reference for Burrator Forest is *568 694*
56 – Can be found in the top and bottom margins of the relevant map sheet (identified at the start of each book section). It is the reference number for one of the grid lines running north/south on the map.
69 – Can be found in the left and right hand margins of the relevant map sheet. It is the reference number for one of the grid lines running east/west on the map.

These numbers locate the bottom left hand corner of the kilometre grid square in which the car park for Burrator Forest appears. The remaining figures of the reference (*568 694*) pinpoint the feature within the grid square to the nearest 100 metres as shown in the diagram below.

The following abbreviations are used:

AONB — Area of outstanding natural beauty
CNT — *County Naturalists' Trust*
CP — Country Park
FC — Forestry Commission
FNR — Forest Nature Reserve
fp — footpath
GLC — Greater London Council
LA — Local Authority
LNR — Local Nature Reserve
MAFF — Ministry of Agriculture Fisheries and Food
NC — Nature Conservancy
NNR — National Nature Reserve
NT — National Trust
NTS — National Trust for Scotland
pf — private forestry
SSSI — Site of Special Scientific Interest
SWT — Scottish Wildlife Trust
WA — Water Authority
WT — Woodland Trust

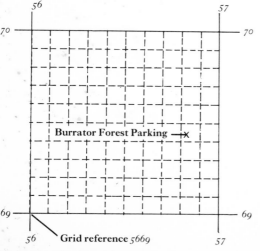

Burrator Forest Parking ➞ ✕

56   Grid reference *5669*   57

The dotted lines within the square do not appear on the face of the map

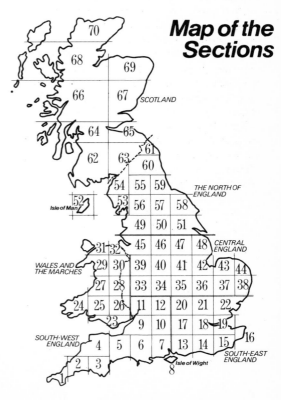

Map of the Sections

SCOTLAND

THE NORTH OF ENGLAND

Isle of Man

WALES AND THE MARCHES

CENTRAL ENGLAND

SOUTH-WEST ENGLAND

Isle of Wight

SOUTH-EAST ENGLAND

1:316,800 maps

RELIEF

Feet	Metres
		·274 Heights in feet above mean sea level
3000	914
2000	610
1400	427
1000	305	Contours at 200ft intervals
600	183
200	61
		To convert feet to metres multiply by 0·3048
0	0

TOURIST INFORMATION

- ✝ Abbey, Cathedral, Priory
- 𝔪 Ancient monument
- Aquarium
- ⋏ Camp site
- Caravan site
- Castle
- Cave
- Country park
- Craft centre
- Garden
- ▶ Golf course or links
- Historic house
- Information centre

- Motor racing
- Museum
- ! Nature or forest trail
- Nature reserve
- ☆ Other tourist feature
- ✕ Picnic site
- Preserved railway
- Racecourse
- Skiing
- Viewpoint
- Wildlife park
- ▲ Youth hostel
- Zoo

ROADS Not necessarily rights of way

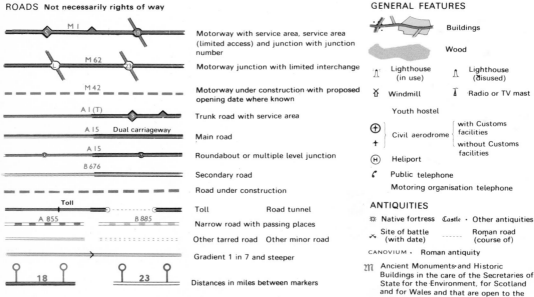

Motorway with service area, service area (limited access) and junction with junction number

Motorway junction with limited interchange

Motorway under construction with proposed opening date where known

Trunk road with service area

Main road

Roundabout or multiple level junction

Secondary road

Road under construction

Toll   Road tunnel

Narrow road with passing places

Other tarred road   Other minor road

Gradient 1 in 7 and steeper

Distances in miles between markers

The representation on this map of a road is no evidence of the existence of a right of way

GENERAL FEATURES

- Buildings
- Wood
- ⋏ Lighthouse (in use)
- ⋏ Lighthouse (disused)
- Windmill
- Radio or TV mast
- Youth hostel
- ⊕ Civil aerodrome { with Customs facilities
- ✚ { without Customs facilities
- Ⓗ Heliport
- ℂ Public telephone
- Motoring organisation telephone

ANTIQUITIES

- ☀ Native fortress   Castle · Other antiquities
- Site of battle (with date)   ------ Roman road (course of)
- CANOVIUM · Roman antiquity
- 𝔪 Ancient Monuments and Historic Buildings in the care of the Secretaries of State for the Environment, for Scotland and for Wales and that are open to the public.

WATER FEATURES

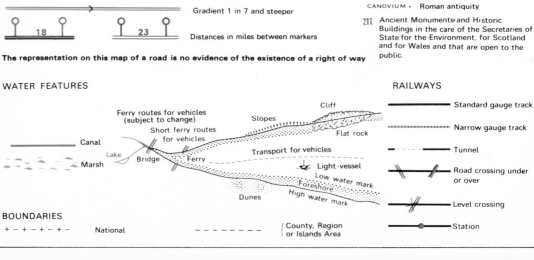

Ferry routes for vehicles (subject to change)
Short ferry routes for vehicles
Cliff
Slopes
Flat rock
Transport for vehicles
Light-vessel
Low water mark
Foreshore
High water mark
Dunes

- Canal
- Lake
- Marsh
- Bridge
- Ferry

RAILWAYS

- Standard gauge track
- Narrow gauge track
- Tunnel
- Road crossing under or over
- Level crossing
- Station

BOUNDARIES

- + – + – + – + – National
- – – – – – – { County, Region or Islands Area

1:50,000 maps

ROADS AND PATHS Not necessarily rights of way

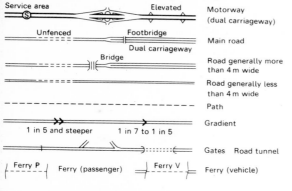

Service area / Elevated	Motorway (dual carriageway)
Unfenced / Footbridge	Main road
Dual carriageway	
Bridge	Road generally more than 4 m wide
	Road generally less than 4 m wide
	Path
	Gradient
1 in 5 and steeper / 1 in 7 to 1 in 5	
	Gates Road tunnel
Ferry P Ferry (passenger) / Ferry V	Ferry (vehicle)

PUBLIC RIGHTS OF WAY (Not applicable to Scotland)

Public rights of way indicated by these symbols have been
derived from Definitive Maps as amended by later enactments
or instruments held by Ordnance Survey on and are shown subject
to the limitations imposed by the scale of mapping

**The representation on this map of any other road, track or
path is no evidence of the existence of a right of way**

TOURIST INFORMATION

🄴	Information centre	✆	Telephone, public/motoring organisation
🄿	Parking	⌐	Golf course or links
P		PC	Public convenience (in rural areas)
✗	Picnic site	☀	Viewpoint

GENERAL FEATURES

	Electricity transmission line (with pylons spaced conventionally)
	Pipe line (arrow indicates direction of flow)
	Buildings
	Public buildings (selected)
	Bus or coach station
Wood	Radio or TV mast
Orchard	Chimney or tower
	Glasshouse
Quarry	Heliport
	Spoil heap, refuse tip or dump
Church or Chapel	with tower
	with spire
	without tower or spire
	Graticule intersection at 5' intervals
△	Triangulation pillar
⊻ Windmill with or without sails	Windpump

HEIGHTS

·144   Heights are to the nearest
metre above mean sea level

Heights shown close to a triangulation pillar refer to the station
height at ground level and not necessarily to the summit.

WATER FEATURES

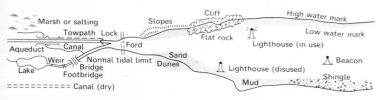

Marsh or salting	Cliff
Towpath Lock	Slopes High water mark
Aqueduct Canal	Flat rock Low water mark
Weir Normal tidal limit	Ford Lighthouse (in use)
Lake Bridge Footbridge	Sand Dunes Beacon
	Lighthouse (disused) Shingle
========= Canal (dry)	Mud

ABBREVIATIONS

P	Post office
PH	Public house
MS	Milestone
MP	Milepost
CH	Clubhouse
PC	Public convenience (in rural areas)
TH	Town Hall, Guildhall or equivalent
CG	Coastguard

BOUNDARIES

— · — · — National	—··—··— County, Region or Islands Area
— ○ — ○ — London Borough	— · — · — District

ANTIQUITIES

VILLA Roman	✕ Battlefield (with date)	+ Position of antiquity which cannot be drawn to scale
Castle Non-Roman	☆ Tumulus	

The revision date of archaeological information varies over the sheet

RAILWAYS

Track multiple or single		Freight line, siding
Track narrow gauge		or tramway
Bridges, Footbridge	Station	
Tunnel	Level crossing	
Viaduct	Embankment	
	Cutting	

HOW TO GIVE A GRID REFERENCE (BRITISH NATIONAL GRID)

100 000 Metre GRID SQUARE IDENTIFICATION	TO GIVE A GRID REFERENCE TO NEAREST 100 METRES
	SAMPLE POINT: The Talbots
	1. Read letters identifying 100 000 metre square in which the point lies. ST
SN | SO 2 00	2. FIRST QUOTE EASTINGS Locate first VERTICAL grid line to LEFT of point and read LARGE figures labelling the line either in the top or bottom margin or on the line itself. Estimate tenths from grid line to point. 05 7
SS | ST	3. AND THEN QUOTE NORTHINGS Locate first HORIZONTAL grid line BELOW point and read LARGE figures labelling the line either in the left or right margin or on the line itself. Estimate tenths from grid line to point. 70 7
3 00	
IGNORE the SMALLER figures of any grid number: these are for finding the full coordinates. Use ONLY the LARGER figure of the grid number. EXAMPLE: 2**69**000m	SAMPLE REFERENCE ST 057 707
	For local referencing grid letters may be omitted.

SOUTH-WEST ENGLAND
West Cornwall

Landranger sheets 203, 204

St Clement Woods, Truro *825 477*, ♀ ♠,
500 acres, 1⅓m, muddy, FC

The car park is well into the trees down a lane from the village of Idless on the northern outskirts of Truro.

This is the first of many Forestry Commission woodlands in this book. The Commission is under a statutory obligation to provide access to its woods and forests, where this will not interfere unduly with young plantations or conflict with other responsibilities – local shooting rights for instance. Capacious and secluded car parks are provided, with picnic areas; 450 of them in Britain. Forest walks and trails are usually waymarked from these places. Leaflet guides are often available. At the more important sites there are toilet facilities. Other activities besides walking are catered for. There are twenty-three Forestry Commission campsites in Britain, mostly excellent and reasonably priced. Disabled people's trails are provided here and there.

It may be objected that providing WCs institutionalizes the atmosphere, and this is true. But much worse is the waste paper and plastic left about by us, the visitors. The Commission does not usually undertake to clear litter, and notices pleading 'Please take your litter home' are irritating: either unnecessary or not complied with.

St Clement Woods have none of these facilities and irritants beyond a decently surfaced car park and careful directions to horse riders to avoid the paths, so that the horses do not churn up the mud. But this wood does show the Commission at its best in integrating softwood production with the broadleaf character of British woodland. The wood is old, as appears at once from its shape on the map: irregular with many concave bays where in the past ploughland has eaten into the wood. Much gorse on the lower levels of the forest road suggests former heathland, not unexpected on higher ground in Cornwall. The prevailing hardwood tree in the wood is hazel.

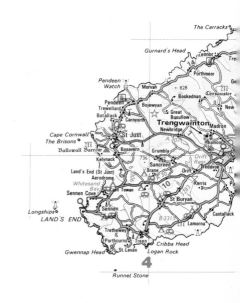

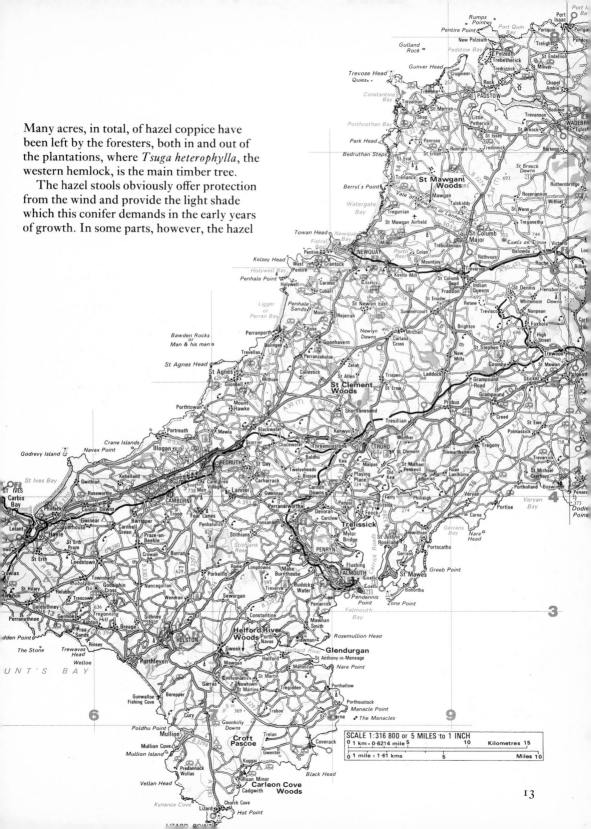

Many acres, in total, of hazel coppice have been left by the foresters, both in and out of the plantations, where *Tsuga heterophylla*, the western hemlock, is the main timber tree.

The hazel stools obviously offer protection from the wind and provide the light shade which this conifer demands in the early years of growth. In some parts, however, the hazel

SCALE 1:316 800 or 5 MILES to 1 INCH

13

coppice is pure. After twenty years of growth the *Tsuga* stands are very dark within, yet the hazel somehow survives. A photograph taken amongst the trees needed one hundred times the exposure required outside.

Tsuga heterophylla – the name means 'varied leaf' and the otherwise rather small, yew-like foliage is easily recognized by the alternating long and short leaves – is here planted in large stands. There are smaller stands of redwoods, unusual in British forestry, but well suited to the mild, frost-free climate here. In their native home, the mist-laden shores of north-west America, they are the world's tallest trees – up to 370 feet. *Eucalyptus* (Australian gum trees), *Nothofagus* (South American beeches), European beech (*Fagus*) and hybrid poplars are also planted. The beech stands are full of bluebells, obviously the original ground cover of the wood: under the conifers are only dead needles and dry twigs.

All this variety makes for interesting walking (or sliding if the weather has been wet: only the central forest road is gravelled and dry). The glory of the place for me is a section of wet

Stitchwort and bluebells, and, TOP, the streamside in St Clement Woods, Truro

oak and sallow woodland which remains by the stream at the east side of the wood. Here the native trees, once coppiced regularly, now sprawl grotesquely, green with moss, holly and honeysuckle amongst them, cowslips and bluebells wherever they can take root beneath. It is a scene of decay, perhaps, but fascinating and decorative. This furthest south-west of the Forestry Commission's woods is well worth visiting.

Carleon Cove *727 157, ♀, 10 minutes' walk, NT*

Of many wooded coves Carleon is car-less, and once contained, uniquely I believe, a wood of pure Cornish elm, *Ulmus angustifolia* var. *stricta* if you follow Melville, or *U. carpinifolia* (*U. stricta*) var. *cornubiensis* according to *The British Flora*. Whatever its name, it is a most distinctive tree and beautiful in every way. The cove now contains the corpses and to me is a very sad place. However, a man walking there was clearly deeply satisfied with the quiet beauty of the place and had not noticed that the trees were dead or that they were elms.

Cadgwith, nearby, has a wood of scrub elm – a hybrid sort, and scrubby because it climbs down a fairly exposed cliff. Again this is a rare phenomenon. The cliff is protected to some extent by a vast natural rock formation called the Devil's Frying-pan. Cadgwith also had many Cornish elms, now all dead. It is still a charming little place with masses of (naturalized) white bluebells, and alexanders along the roadsides nearly as bright as the yellow lines.

Inland are Goonhilly Downs, bleak but lovable, with a dark, dramatic patch of Sitka spruce in the middle, contrasting beautifully with the clean shells of the several satellite-tracking aerials. This lonely forest, Croft Pascoe, is a Forestry Commission experiment which seems to be succeeding.

North of Goonhilly are the wooded shores of the Helford River, from Gweek, far from bleak, to Durgan, a village with no road outwards, only inwards. Glendurgan, with famous subtropical gardens belonging to the National Trust, is probably magnificent, but unfortunately I always arrive on a Tuesday or a Thursday or at a weekend, none of these times being suitable.

Trengwainton, Penzance *445 313, ♀ ♣, easy, ⅔m total, NT*

Penzance is a plant experience in itself; the town park, though not a woodland, is full of palms, tree ferns, myrtle and gorgeous rhododendrons. See the fine row of cabbage trees in the Memorial Garden. (These branching palm trees from New Zealand

TAMARISK
Distinctively Cornish hedges of this feathery, yellow-green import from Europe, *Tamarix gallica*, now naturalized as *T. anglica*, produce bits of very hard timber for boat repairs and tool handles. Some trees are now old pollards. Hard winters strip the evergreen foliage, leaving spiky skeletons, but all grow again during the following year. Flowers are dull pink sprays, supposedly whiter in *T. gallica*.

actually flower here in great sprays of tiny florets – even in people's back gardens.)

Trengwainton is a great garden and its walled compartments contain many rare and extremely beautiful plants: among trees are very fine magnolias and a *Tsuga canadensis* variety which sprawls over an old wall. The driveway up to the house is planted with equally rare and impressive trees: *Davidia*, perhaps not so rare but splendid here; a line of real tree ferns, *Dicksonia antarctica*; the rare *Nothofagus moorei*; several *Eucalyptus* species,

and at the top a fine old *Cephalotaxus* (horribly named the Chinese cow's tail pine) with purple, peeling bark. All the way the trees are luxurious in foliage and fine in form. On the horizon is a line of Monterey pines.

Trelissick *836 396*, ♀ ♣, *3m or shorter options, NT*

Another famous garden, Trelissick, has a perimeter Woodland Walk, so described, which is always open. You can start near the King Harry Ferry where the notice invites you, or from the house. Actually, it is dull, except for the ships in the Fal and some more open, less overgrown, parts of the footpath. Parking at the house is free.

Across the ferry you can drive through the Lamorran Woods and some of the Penkevil Woods deep in their coombes: oak, beech and ash in unusual magnificence, *Rhododendron arboreum* and swans in the dammed-up Lamorran inlet.

Beeches by the Fal Estuary, Trelissick

There are many other wooded lowlands in south Cornwall: less in the north, but St Mawgan, with its very characteristic church in a bowl filled with trees and with a wooded valley upstream, is attractive. Many tiny wooded coombes inland from this north-west coast are not large enough to provide woodland walks but they are so pretty that I must mention them. You have only to drive off the main routes for a few minutes to be transported into a sort of fairyland of native trees, bushes and flowers. Many hedge banks by the sea are crowned with lines of tamarisk.

Bodmin and East Cornwall

Landranger sheets 190, 200, 201

SCALE 1:316 800 or 5 MILES to 1 INCH

0 1 km = 0·6214 mile 5   10   Kilometres 15

0 1 mile = 1·61 kms   5   Miles 10

Between Bodmin and Wadebridge is a quiet countryside of narrow lanes, banked with flowers, in and out of deep valleys. Some very fine woods are here all coniferized but not less dramatic for that, and retain some old features and boundaries. There are no Forestry Commission car parks but access is perfectly easy.

Hawkes Wood ♀, *9 acres, NNR*, Treneague Woods *985 715*, ♣, *1½m along valley, FC*

From the centre of Wadebridge turn down by the Bridge on Wool pub, and go ¾ mile to the crossroads where a signpost points to St Breock. Take the small road opposite to this, up and then down into the valley of the stream – a few yards only. Here you may well admire the patch of beech and sycamore over the stream, the banks snowed under with wild garlic, more than the rather grim-looking Forestry Commission entrance opposite. But tramp up the forest road at least for ¼ mile to see the fine oaks of the small nature reserve, also noted for its ferns (in a disused quarry) and varied bird population. Whether this includes hawks I do not know. Look out for fine bracket fungus on trees by the road.

Hustyn Wood and Bishop's Wood
005 697, ♣, *500 acres, forest roads, FC*
This plantation is just magnificent. Forest roads are open, and, since everyone makes for the coast, there are few visitors.

A Camel Valley Walk *015 681*, ♀ ♣,
metalled road or fp, 1¾m, FC
The parking place indicated will take one car and you can cross the footbridge at Brocton to reach a footpath which follows an old railway; this, however, leads you out of the woodland. You can walk in the Forestry Commission woods, but it is uphill and not very promising. My walk is along the lane towards Ruthernbridge, conifers on one side, native streamside vegetation on the other. It is a very quiet lane. Walking back, you see everything the other way round. I know it sounds vague for a walk, but on a fine summer's morning it is perfect.

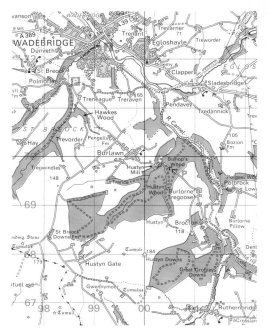

The road through Hustyn Wood

Dunmere Wood *043 688*, ♀ ♣, *at least 750 acres, FC*
This great wood, on a hill and down to the Camel Valley just north of Bodmin, is an old oakwood now converted into slabs of alternate beech and spruce by the Forestry Commission. There ought to be proper access so that one might at least find some traces of its past, for it is well known; but there is nowhere to park and I am told there is no plan for a car park in the foreseeable future.

EAST AND SOUTH OF BODMIN

Lavethan Wood, Blisland *104 729*, ♀, *25 acres, easy, ½m, WT*

From the ugly Bodmin Moor of the A30(T), Blisland is like heaven (Helland is the next village). Blisland has a triangular green surrounded by cottages in strict Georgian style, except for the post office, which is Cornish abstract art. Blisland also has a wood, in a valley bottom to the south: beech and oak with yew, invaded by sycamore and rhododendron. Great work is being done in coppicing the rhododendron and there is much natural regeneration of the native trees – not that this will get rid of the rhododendron. This is a faultless woodland walk; but take your wellies – it is a bridleway too.

Hart Wood *098 642, FC*, ## Lanhydrock Park *NT*

It is often difficult or impossible to arrange a round walk without taking in miles of road or fields. As I see it, my task is first to find your wood.

Take the second by-road right after the roundabout on the Bodmin to Liskeard road, A38(T), for Hart Wood, *103 639*, which has a small woodland walk through oaks and flowers, then larches and spruces. Across the road (at the map reference), through a red gate, is a driveway by the riverside to Bodmin Road Station. Here are fine old oaks and yews by the river, while along the drive are mighty specimens of Victorian conifer favourites, notably a well-shaped Lawson cypress, and many others. This is part of a 1¾-mile carriage drive from Lanhydrock House to the station, seemingly rather an expensive addition to the owner's first-class season ticket; but when you see the size of the estate you realize it must have been a relatively small item.

The drive, interrupted by a short stretch of roadway, continues to the house over parkland. Car parking, *085 636*, for the house and park is at the north-west side. The great lines of Lanhydrock's beeches are landscape features, visible from the trunk road, grander and more impressive as you come closer. Functionally essential shelter-belts for this hilltop estate,

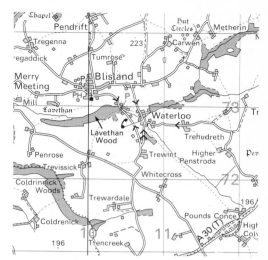

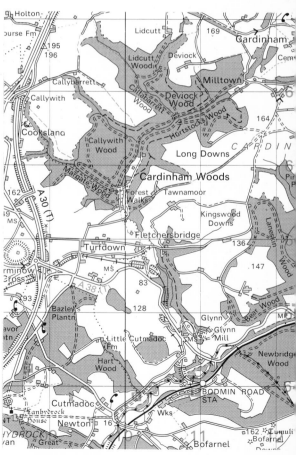

Lanhydrock shelter-belt

Cardinham Woods: a Glynn Valley viewpoint

they have great architectural quality – beautifully massed and balanced. Even the parking place is like the nave of a great cathedral. You can walk all round the park under the beech trees. Who would have thought that prosaic-sounding Bodmin Road Station could lead to all this? The best approach is surely by that forgotten, sequestered driveway with its avenue of Victorian conifers.

Cardinham Woods 099 667, (♀) ⚹, *1000 acres, 4 walks and trails, FC*

The steep-sided, deep valleys of streams, particularly the Glynn, which drain the southern slopes of Bodmin Moor were almost certainly oak-covered before human settlement and then coppiced until cleared and planted by the Forestry Commission. But admiration of this now Canadian landscape leaves little room for regret at the loss of native heritage. Alders, willows, oaks and beeches can, anyway, still keep a foothold by the streams and margins, and there is an impressive group of oaks as you drive in: be thankful! (The turning off the A38 to Liskeard from Bodmin is a few hundred yards after the roundabout, signposted Fletchersbridge.)

You could spend days in this romantic place, where Douglas fir and Sitka spruce grow 100 feet in thirty years. At the least you can drive through the Glynn Valley, pausing to look back where a small stopping place has been made, and then nosing out through tiny lanes to a fine gorse common on Long Downs.

There are several other large woods to explore towards Liskeard. To the south the Forestry Commission's **Deerpark Trail**, *198 604*, follows forest roads and paths in what is described as a typical Cornish wooded valley – 'with oak coppice and silver-fir plantations'. Deerpark Wood is on a tributary stream of the West Looe River, itself wooded all the way down to West Looe.

Northwards, on Bodmin Moor, is the enormous 1000-acre plantation of Smallacombe Downs, as yet mysterious and inaccessible. The only slightly smaller **Halvana Plantation**, more mature, is close to the A30 and has a picnic place at *215 788* and a waymarked walk of $1\frac{1}{2}$ miles of spruce and pine, with moorland mining relics and good views. Turn south at Fivelanes.

Mount Edgecumbe 453 533 and 446 521, ♀ ⚹, *96 acres, 3m or much less, CP*

The Mount was named by the Edgecumbe family who moved in the seventeenth century to the grand mansion here from Cotehele, their ancestral home on the Tamar. In 1816 a local journalist described Edgecumbe as 'that other

Devonshire from Cornwall: Plymouth and Dartmoor from Mount Edgecumbe

Eden', referring presumably only to its landscape. It has a very good view of Devonshire and retains a dense belt of woodland round the deer park – as well as numerous follies, a Grand Avenue etc. The parking place at Cremyll is a bit towny; the other, by the lonely church on the hill, is attractive. The important tree at Edgecumbe is the beech, but there are natural-looking oaks as well, mostly over a hundred years old and very picturesque. Before being caught in a squall I explored part of Drywalk Wood, on the north-facing slopes of the park. It was far from dry, the paths badly overgrown with rhododendron gone jungly. There were some acres of new-planted beech; and the thickest patches of bluebells I have seen since childhood, the intense blue haze broken only by the narrow pathways of deer.

The great attraction is the coastal path, through woodland, which I failed to explore. I had hoped to cross by the pedestrian ferry to Cremyll, but could see no sign of it from the Plymouth shore. Going by the car ferry was time consuming, but not too expensive, and the road brings you to the hilltop.

This is a very successful Country Park, the only one in Cornwall. It is fine parkland – the woodland is incidental – and it is worth a day's outing.

Boscastle: St Peter's Wood *119 905,* ♀, *(Minster Church), fp, wooded valley, 50 acres, NNR*
Valency Valley *300 acres, NT*
St Peter's Wood, with sessile oak, is on the north side of the valley, all of which belongs to the National Trust. You can also park near the main road opposite the Cobweb Inn, and walk up the heavily wooded valley.

SOUTH-WEST ENGLAND
Dartmoor

Landranger sheets 191, 192, 201, 202

Looking across the tree-filled Bovey Valley

DARTMOOR FOREST

The moors (poor grass, heather, bracken, gorse and peat) occupy the western half of the compact 365-square-mile blob-shaped National Park. In the middle are three great conifer forests. The eastern side of the blob (which is a block of granite) is largely hill-farming country, broken by the three wooded valleys of the Teign, the Bovey and the Dart (and its tributaries). The Lyd Gorge is to the west.

Three very small oakwoods remain in the high moors. Perhaps they are fragments of greater woods long ago; but their origins are mysterious. Much of the moorland is common land and as such must have been grazed for centuries unrecorded – before it ever came to be called a forest. Deer and the commoners' animals – sheep and ponies – have seen to it

that very few trees indeed in the 120,000 acres of moorland have ever had a chance of natural reproduction. The moorland woods survive probably because they grow among boulders, which break the sheep's legs, and perhaps improve the drainage locally, rather like pieces of broken pottery in the bottom of a plant pot. Part of one of the remote Dartmoor woods, Wistman's Wood, fenced off as an experiment from 1965, is full of sweet grasses, brambles, bilberries – and tree seedlings. The steep valley side opposite another high-moorland oakwood, Piles Copse, has rowan, hawthorn, whitebeam, oaks and a holly tree: in fact, trees are seeded and thrive here, miles of bare semi-desert all around, because the oakwood attracts birds and the bit of land in question is too steep for even a mountain sheep. The copse itself, pure sessile oak and not in fact coppiced, grows characteristically on mossy boulder scree but is

continuously grazed, the boulders being fairly
small with few crevasses. It is a safe bet (the
wood was inaccessible to me across the
flooding river) that there are no oak seedlings
there. The origins of Wistman's Wood, long
famous for its weirdly contorted, moss–hung
trees, are even more obscure, for it consists
entirely of pedunculate oak, some trees very
old, where sessile oak would be expected.

Dartmoor oaks in Wistman's Wood.
TOP: Black Tor Copse, RIGHT: Piles Copse.

Wistman's Wood, Two Bridges

609 750, ♀, 63 acres, 2m, FNR
You have to walk for a mile northwards from
the hotel at Two Bridges, near Princetown.
The wood is signposted at the cottage ¼ mile
from the gate. Gumboots are essential except
in high summer.

Piles Copse, Torr *625 612, ♀, about 40*

acres, 2½m, FNR
The map reference is a parking place just on
the moorland. The wood is 1¼ miles north-

east. A permit is required from the Water Authority if you cross their land, but you can follow the waymarked path around it. This route, from Cornwood and Torr, brings you to the west bank of the River Erme, opposite the wood; the river may be impossible to cross after rain. But you get a very good view of the wood, and can examine the natural growth on the near side, mentioned above.

Black Tor Copse, Meldon *562 918*, ♀, *about 50 acres, 4m, FNR, Army Danger Area*

The only access is from the excellent parking place (the map reference) at the dam of Meldon Reservoir, clearly signposted from the village. The wood is 2 miles south-south-west. Take the bridleway signposted 'To the Moors and Sourton', but follow an old contour path which branches off before the line of beeches. At the head of the reservoir cross the arched bridge and the wet plain: continue up the West Okement River. A notice gives clear instructions about warning flags, but only after you have covered $1\frac{1}{2}$ miles of rough country.

Each of these woods requires a non-woodland walk in well-soled gumboots: each is well worth the effort. The walk to Wistman's is dull, but the other two are not just walks; they are experiences: of water, rocks and space, as well as of trees.

These oakwood curiosities are minute compared with the Forestry Commission's transformations of the moorland scenery.

Fernworthy Forest *669 839, (♀)* ♣, *1600 acres, forest trails, FC*

The superb stands of forestry conifers are spread in a vast arc over the several moorland valleys which drain into the Fernworthy Reservoir. In the wide, wet margins of the water, sheltered on all sides by the plantations, a rich sallow woodland has developed. Amongst the pines and the spruces are many ancient standing stones, hut circles and cairns. The setting is superlative and the approach road (west from Chagford) climbs dramatically to moorland from beautiful wooded farmland, between massive stone hedges crowned with

beeches. North of the forest is **Gidleigh Common**, a Site of Special Scientific Interest, with scattered trees amongst hut circles and beautiful views over the lowlands.

Bellever Forest *652 771*, ♣, *1300 acres, waymarked trail with options, FC*

The forest looks complicated on the map, not quite filling the spaces between the road, the B3212, the East Dart River, and Bellever village and Bellever Tor (1453 feet) but it looks very well shaped from the surrounding high moors – a lesson in landscaping to answer the critics of conifer plantations. The car park is a bit dark and forbidding. A map identifies the areas occupied by various species: Douglas fir, silver fir, Japanese larch and Sitka spruce. Sitka and Japanese larches are the oldest trees here, planted in 1921: they look very big. *Pinus contorta*, the lodgepole pine, is also used.

The forest produces about £350,000 worth of timber a year and also has given a home to the first breeding siskins in Devon. The old Lych Way through the forest was used by church-goers to Lydford; the dead were carried to burial over some 10 miles of moor and valley. The Way is now suffering from too much trampling. The third large area of planting by the Forestry Commission is at Soussons Down, $1\frac{1}{2}$ miles north-east of and practically part of the Bellever Forest.

Burrator Forest *568 694*, ♀ ♣, *1000 acres, paths and a forest road, WA*

The gleaming water with its tree-clad slopes, close to Yelverton, is an attractive focus for sightseers. Statistics of the Dartmoor National Park Authority show that of all visitors to Dartmoor, 29 per cent never leave their car, 35 per cent stray only 100 yards and 34 per cent go about a mile. Walking only 200 yards from the main car park here brings you to a typical Dartmoor oakwood on boulders, by a loud stream, and all covered in vivid green moss. A mile takes you into varied conifer country, much of it mature woodland, and to the moors.

Very popular is the Water Authority's Burrator Reservoir, surrounded by softwood plantations nicely arranged with considerable leeway for native trees.

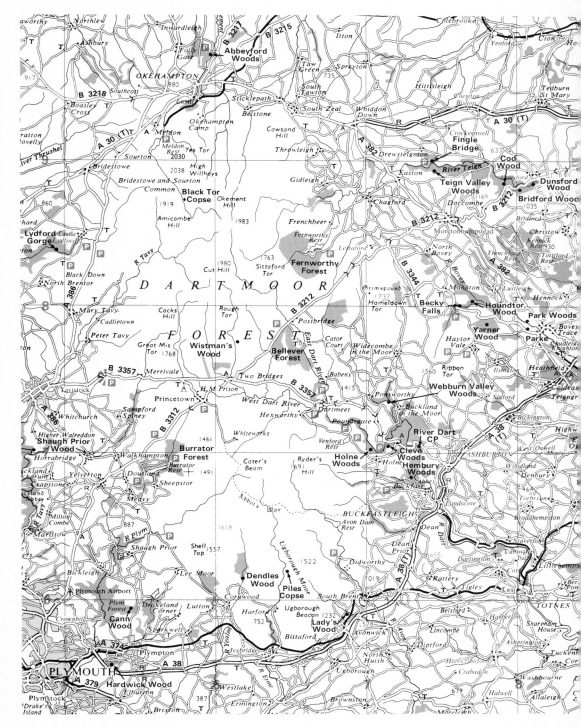

DARTMOOR VALLEY WOODS

These are numerous and complex and would require a whole guidebook of their own. Taking the main wooded valleys in clockwise order, starting at 1 o'clock:

Teign Valley Woods 743 899, ♀ ♣, 1500 acres, fp, 8m, pf, NT

The map reference gives an awkward, steep access point for a car, Fingle Bridge, but which at least takes you into the middle of the dark, conifer-clad valleys, via photogenic Drewsteignton and close to the fast A30(T). At the upper end of the valley are National Trust woodlands dominated by the grandiose Castle Drogo. A footpath to Fingle Bridge begins on the Drewsteignton to Sandy Park road, just to the north-west of Castle Drogo's hill. At the lower end **Dunsford Wood, Cod Wood** and the National Trust **Bridford Wood**, well known for daffodils, lie across the Moretonhampstead road from Exeter. There is a nature trail here at 804 883.

Choose your route at Becka Falls

Becka Falls and Houndtor Wood, Manaton 757 800, ♀ ♣, 300yds or 3m, pf

This is a beauty spot, and it *is* beautiful. Parking is free and there is a café. There are steps down to the view of the falls, where children may leap fairly safely from rock to rock. Fine, mossy oaks have wall pennywort as well as ferns growing up their trunks. Of many silver-stemmed hollies, not one seems to have escaped being engraved with people's initials. Following the valley-side path downstream

brings you to a small hazel coppice, where the trees, despairing of ever being cut again, are throwing up new shoots of their own accord. The path goes on by hemlock and western red cedar plantations, but with primroses, and you soon reach a fourways signpost where you must choose your route, long or short.

Yarner Wood 785 793, ♀, 450 acres, walk 3½m or shorter, nature trail, NR

This is a good example of a valley oakwood and is carefully managed to provide the maximum range of habitat and to produce wood for fencing etc. Some years ago the pied flycatchers left the wood because of a shortage, not of food, but of suitable holes to nest in. As with other oakwoods around Dartmoor there are few old trees. Nest-boxes were provided and the pied flycatchers returned.

The nature trail delights everyone. What I would have thought impossible is here achieved with style: the provision of museum showcases, waterproofed with felt, amongst the trees. One case describes and illustrates with models the habits of the wood ant. Very good; but what rivets the visitor is a real, active community of wood ants opposite the showcase. No wonder there are entries like TERRIFIC in the visitors' book.

The oldest trees here are a row of beeches, their silver trunks beautifully marked with lichen. The walks are carefully signposted and not difficult.

A mile north-west of Bovey Tracey off the Manaton road is **Parke**, 805 785, the local headquarters of the National Trust and the Dartmoor National Park Authority. Here are an Interpretation Centre – posh name for a bookstall – and a Bovey Valley Walk under beeches, a mile or so if you just cross the bridge into Parke Wood, or nearly 3 miles if you go up through Ledge Wood, by the Rare Breeds Farm, and cross the river by the road.

Holne Woods and Cleve Wood 705 695, Holne, 711 709, New Bridge, ♀ ♣, riverside walks of optional length, NT (Holne Woods)

The New Bridge car park is busy and you may prefer to park in Holne village and walk by the signed footpath over two fields down into the

In the Dart Valley in early summer

woods; this route will show you from above what you are about to plunge into – and will fill your lungs with air. Gumboots are essential.

Turn left at the river path for the exquisite beeches of Holne Woods. Words will not describe their perfection. On the way there are lots of sycamore and rhododendron escaped from jealously guarded estates above. The rhododendrons are, mercifully, being cut, but of course *Rhododendron ponticum* coppices like the devil and is extremely difficult to uproot.

The whole of the Dart Valley woodlands, over 900 acres, are 'dedicated', either belonging to the Devon Trust for Nature Conservation or the National Trust, from *672 731* north, to *708 704* south, and there are several access points, from the (most-visited) car park at Dartmeet downwards.

Blackadon Tor and Webburn Valley Woods *712 732 (entrance)*, ♀ ♣, *steep, often muddy, NR*
Moorland with bracken and birches above, mixed pedunculate and sessile oaks below and some beeches by the river – an ash coppice to the south, with coppiced sycamore. This

nature reserve is on a bend of the River Webburn, which is a tributary of the Dart. You can just park in the entrance lane which is below and opposite the attractive Leusdon Lodge Hotel; otherwise there is plenty of room on the fine Leusdon Common (a Site of Special Scientific Interest).

A little way towards Widecombe-in-the-Moor is Ponsworthy, where a footpath 'To Jordans', *701 739*, goes up the West Webburn stream through a pretty wood full of ferns and flowers. This is a muddy path but there is no climb to do, except that, returning, you may find a path a few feet higher on the valley side.

At Ashburton, a cramped little town which seems to catch many holidaymakers, the **River Dart Country Park** is signposted. In its 23 acres, *734 701*, it accommodates a busy residential centre running outdoor courses for children – it all looks very exciting – self-catering holidays for grown-ups, camping, swimming, riding, fishing, tennis, 'jungle fun', and has a picnic meadow, an adventure playground, a shop, a tree trail and even a quiet woodland walk by the river. Parking was fairly costly.

Hembury Woods

SOUTH AND WEST OF DARTMOOR

Hembury Woods *728 680, ♀, 374 acres, steep in places, NT*
By contrast the National Trust Hembury, to the south, is peaceful and asks only for a ten-pence donation. It is a very beautiful oakwood and there is a walk down to the river with beeches (15 minutes) or up to Hembury Castle among birches – a stiff climb. The parking and picnic place, *728 680*, struck me as one of the most lovely places I had ever visited, the fairly young (sixty years) oaks decorated with lichen and ivy and the whole place dotted with the blue of bluebells and the yellow of broom which grow between the oaks. There is a lot of bramble away from this pleasant grassy patch.

To reach Hembury, go out of Buckfast in the direction of Scorriton but fork right, not signposted, instead of left to Scorriton and Holne.

Lady's Wood, Ugborough *685 594, ♀, 8 acres, easy but damp, NR*
Park by the charming bridge on a minor road from South Brent to Cheston, signposted Owley. This is a depressing little wood of oak and ash over hazel and holly, much overgrown in spite of supposedly being coppiced on a seven-compartment cycle. But I suppose on a fine morning it could be heavenly. Trains rush over a viaduct.

It is incredible to think that Ivybridge was once a well-known beauty-spot around 1800, painted by Turner as the essence of perfect peace. Woods north of Cornwood are Sites of Special Scientific Interest including **Dendles Wood**, *615 618*, but Dendles Waste is a heavy block of conifers.

Shaugh Prior Wood on the River Meavy, *534 636*, is also a Site of Special Scientific Interest. **Hardwick Wood**, *530 555*, belonging to the Woodland Trust, is practically in

Plymouth. There is a forest walk in **Cann Wood**, *545 595*, which is coniferous – the Forestry Commission's Plym Beat, so called. This is rather difficult to find because of poor signposting in Plympton: take the Shaugh Prior road. The forest walk was closed when I eventually found it.

The National Trust **Lydford Gorge** is well known with great trees in nearly subtropical mist from the waterfall. There is a charge for parking. **Lydford Forest**, *489 845*, Forestry Commission, has a forest trail.

Ancient oak trees at Meavy, just in the Park at the west, and at Teigngrace just outside at the south-east, have been preserved for sentiment, otherwise old trees and old coppice stools are nowhere to be seen on or near Dartmoor. The oldest trees in the Dartmoor Forest are in Wistman's Wood, hardly more than 10 feet high. Was the Dartmoor Forest once a great oakwood? I do not know, but I am quite sure that the pathetically small remains on the moors should be allowed to increase naturally by the simple erection of fences.

But as you emerge from the woods once more to the bare, brown moor you breathe deeply and exclaim again what a very beautiful place it is. No wonder 8 million people come to see it every year.

NORTH OF DARTMOOR

Abbeyford Woods *590 976*, ♀ ⚲, *500 acres, 2 forest walks, total 2½m, easy, FC*
The woods begin hardly a mile north of Okehampton – turn off the B3217 – and the parking place is well into the trees along the road which bisects the woodland: beech and conifers of various ages. This is an attractive, quiet wood with, it is said, a wide range of bird life.

NEAR KINGSBRIDGE

Avon Valley Woods *736 509 to 732 483*, ♀, *2m, easy, wet, WT*
Avon is pronouced here with a short 'a'. Finding the south end of the walk at Loddiswell's old railway station is not easy.

You should be on the east bank of the river on the road to Woodleigh. The wood is not all that marvellous, but its wet carpet of flowers is; here wild garlic or ramsons predominates, and there is yellow archangel, lugubriously named *Galeobdolon*, a sort of yellow deadnettle, amongst the anemones, bluebells and primroses. The disused railway is an alternative and parallel path. What a railway this must have been, deep in the valley woods!

At the north or upstream end there is nowhere to park near Topsham Bridge and you have to squeeze in to the roadside where a gate leads to a private driveway. The Woodland

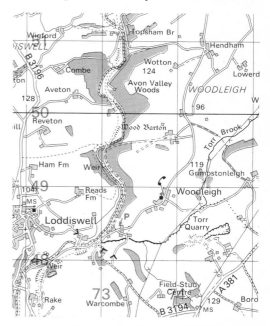

Ground cover in the Avon Valley Woods

Trust obviously intends one to use this drive.
Head downhill at the first opportunity. The
bluebells at this end of the wood are
magnificent. There is a lot of sycamore but
soon you come to some fine beeches. It is very
quiet except for the laughing of the Avon.

EXETER

Great Haldon *897 840* and **Mamhead** *922 805*, (♀), ♠

Familiar to drivers from Exeter to Plymouth
on the A38(T) is the noble shape of the forested Great Haldon, 3 miles from the end of the
motorway, M5. There are three parking places,
with waymarked walks, in this large forest, and
the road to the appropriately Scottish-
sounding Dunchideock, signposted from the
trunk road, goes through the woodland for 2
miles to the Lawrence Tower. Views are
enormous through the dignified ranks of fine
Scots pines, while the road is bordered by a
great beech hedge grown up into an avenue.
Great Haldon is impressive, almost
overwhelming, and needs plenty of time to
be explored.

From the A380 Torquay road, you can get
to the Obelisk at the Forestry Commission's
Mamhead picnic place, *921 808*, again with
magnificent views, here taking in the Exe
Estuary and the Blackdown Hills.

Great Haldon

Very close to Exeter, **Stoke Woods** have a
Forestry Commission picnic place on the A396
to Tiverton. The walk here is in mature
oakwoods and younger forestry plantation.

Close to the motorway and north-east of

Exeter are **Killerton House and Park** and
Ashclyst Forest. Killerton, National Trust, is
famous and much visited for its garden. All its
trees are fine specimens (well formed as trees
commonly are in Devonshire vales) and the
park woods are open when the house and
garden are not. Besides the rather uncomfort-
ably sloping car park inside the main gates you
can enter near the Culm Bridge on the road to
Silverton (B3185). Here there is difficulty in
parking. The path has a National Trust sign to
Columbjohn.

Exeter University grounds are in 300 acres
once belonging to the famous seedsmen Veitch
& Co, and are full of interesting trees.

Ashclyst Forest *000 995*, ♀ ♠, *1250 acres, 3 waymarked walks, muddy, NT, FC*

Clyst is a river name, common in this enviably
mild and long-settled Devonshire countryside
– perhaps meaning an especially clear stream.
Ashclyst is a very attractive forest, a landscape
of great variety, interest and charm. The
woods are managed by the Forestry
Commission for the National Trust, with
perhaps a little too much compromising
towards timber production. One may ask, is it
the job of the National Trust to produce
softwood timber? One advantage however is
that clear-felled areas let in the sky and give
views of beautifully shaped oaks, birches and
ash trees that one would not otherwise have.
The cleared areas, besides adding to the poetry
of the scene, provide variety of habitat. Purist
arguments cannot apply, for the woods already
contain conifers planted a long time ago – such
as an almost ancient Sitka spruce (the tree was
introduced to Britain in 1831) by the road.

The map reference is for the Forest Gate
parking place, very pleasant and with a notice-
board map showing the extent of the various
walks. I am afraid I soon got lost, because
trackways were often impassable through deep
mud – this was an extraordinarily wet spring.

White Down Copse and **Paradise Copse**,
through deep, narrow lanes to the north, are
also National Trust and managed partly for
softwoods. All were part of the Killerton Estate
until 1944.

North Cornwall, North Devon and Exmoor Landranger sheets 180, 181, 190

Kilkhampton: Coombe Valley Woods
208 116, ♀, 1½m, wooded valley, NT
The woods arise ¼ mile inland: oaks at first
child-high, then rapidly building up in lovely
wind-cut curves which fill the fold of the quiet
valley. Above on the hill some parabolic dish
aerials have a similar perfection of form,
arrived at less empirically. In the empty lower
valley where the small trees begin, a boy sat on
a gate, alone and motionless in the wind and
sun – a poetic moment.

The Forestry Commission has a picnic place
here, and has probably cleared a few thousand
beautiful oaks, but has been discreet. A nature
trail is run in conjunction with the County
Naturalists' Trust.

**The Hobby Drive, Clovelly: Hobby
Lodge** *336 234, ♀, 1½m, wooded cliff, pf*
You have to pay to take a car, but not too
much. The drive finishes just north-west of
Clovelly, where the paved footpath descends to
the village. The trees are fascinating,
particularly beeches, twisted but large and with
richly patterned trunks. There are places to
stop along the drive.

Buck's Mills Wood *357 234, ♀, 23 acres,
inaccessible, WT*
Towards Bideford from Clovelly it is the slight
shelter of the north-facing bay which means
that woods can clothe the cliffs. The Woodland
Trust has done a great service by preserving
this section of oakwood with its ferns and
bluebells, but it is too early to talk of access –
which I found to my great discomfort. It is so
full of the wandering stems of brambles and so
steep that it is almost impossible to get from
one side to the other; adjacent woods are
similar. There is a Forestry Commission car

Buck's Mills Wood and Barnstaple Bay

park on the opposite side of the valley with a short woodland walk, and this is our map reference. Apart from this car park, everything is rather cramped and the little place could be swamped on a busy day. Once on the cliff top – via steps past the cottages of the coastguard lookout – the view of Barnstaple Bay and Lundy Island is splendid.

Inland there are two Forestry Commission plantations of considerable interest:

Melbury Woods *364 191, ♣, 1000 acres plus, forest trail, FC*

The land south-east of Woolsery (sometimes spelt Woolfardisworthy) is low and marshy, and the plantations of spruce and pine are richly embroidered with sallows – all doing much, one feels, to improve the ground. The place seemed very remote and silent on a fine Sunday in May.

Hartland Forest: Welsford and Summerwell Woods *278 211, ♣, 350 acres plus, 1½m trail and others, FC*

Here the slowly undulating brown moorland is cut by marshy streams feeding the Upper Torridge, and lined with grey willows – a painter's colours: the broad strokes of dark green conifers complete the colour scheme be the sky grey or blue. This is a forest for

In the Hartland Forest

striding through, or even driving through (very slowly): a fine visual experience not added to by the tatty 'scientific' display at the Information Centre. Avoid it, avoid the trail, wander and enjoy the clean, scented air, the distances, the dark, rich colours.

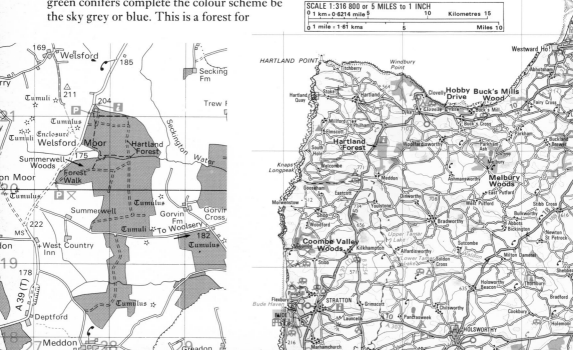

Holsworthy Woods *353 018,* ♣,
450 acres, trail, FC
A cramped parking place and a sad forest of
spruces which fall over because the roots
cannot strike deep enough in the clay.

Arlington Court *614 408,* ♀ ♣, *3500 acres
(not all woodland),* $1\frac{1}{2}m$ *or more, NT*
It must have looked just the same a hundred
years ago, except that the monkey puzzles
would be much smaller. The walk round the

park takes in an avenue of these mighty trees
and then descends to the lake where older oaks
and beeches are reflected. Determined walkers
can then add a couple of miles or so to Loxhore
Cott, by a stream which laps the feet of
coppiced oaks, or, less energetic, may climb up
again through the shady Wilderness of much
rhododendron, redwoods, and a Japanese cedar
to a smaller lake with impressive *Gunnera*
producing enormous flower spikes in spring.
There is a large, red *Rhododendron arborea* on

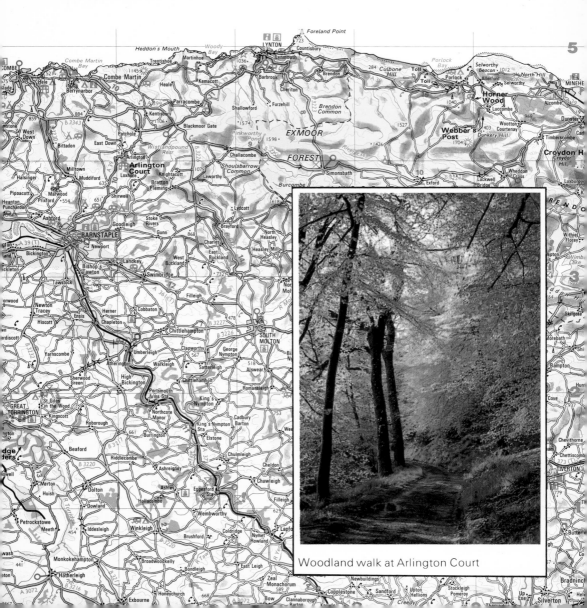

Woodland walk at Arlington Court

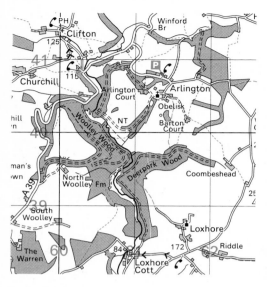

Exmoor pine. OPPOSITE: Horner Hill

the lawn between the house and the church, and this also needs to be seen in spring – these apart, this would be a good walk for a hot summer's day.

Torridge meanders: an undiscovered walk, *537 138*, ♣, *pf*
There are paths along the east bank marked on the map but I was not able to discover a recommendable means of access, there was no one to ask, and I was too busy photographing the marvellous view. It seems a remarkably scenic and little-frequented region, south-east of Torrington. I must leave it at that.

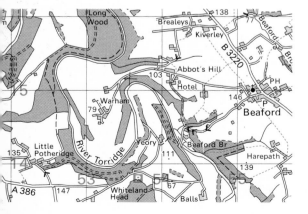

EXMOOR AND THE BRENDON HILLS

Rising dark to the east of the Torr and the Yeo, Exmoor Forest is as bald as the Forest of Rossendale in Lancashire, and it can be bleaker in winter. Simonsbath Farm, the first to be made on Exmoor, contained in 1814 four ash trees, three large beeches, twenty-three sycamores and seven lime pollards; in all, thirty-seven trees. Forestation of the moors was considered, then given up, and the forest was enclosed, small lots being given to commoners – no substitute for their ancient roving grazing rights. The warden got 3000 acres and the Crown 10,000, which it sold for £60,000. Heroic attempts were made by the buyers, the Knight family of ironmasters, to create farmland, but the old rump remains, bare, and, to many, beautiful in its barrenness.

In a forest so forbidding to trees we can make no pretence here to study the moorland. I have also missed the coastal valleys of **Lynton** and **Lynmouth**, and, less forgivably, the **Heddon Valley**, *655 482*, and **Woody Bay, Martinhoe**, *675 487*, a total together of over 1000 acres of National Trust land: woodland, moorland and cliffs.

Horner Wood and Webber's Post

899 455, ♀, ♠ (Horner village), 903 437
(Webber's Post), many routes, 2–4m,
NT etc

Dunkery Hill belongs to the National Trust,
and the Beacon, 1705 feet, is the highest point
on Exmoor. Horner Water flows out
northwards to Porlock Bay through the deepest
of shadowy coombes, filled with native oaks.
The road over the moors to Exford at first
follows the tributary of the Horner, East
Water. There is a large parking place in this
valley at Cloutsham, among fine woods of
durmast oak. At Webber's Post and on Horner
Hill are pinewoods diversified with birch and
holly; gorse and bracken on the slopes.
Remarkably, the hollies are cropped into
rounded bushes. It is said that only pure-bred
Exmoor ponies can survive a hard winter here
– they must be the ones with the hardest
mouths.

You can start a walk from Porlock or from
Horner, either following the stream on the
west bank or climbing Horner Hill. A short
section along the road links the footbridge over
East Water with Webber's Post.

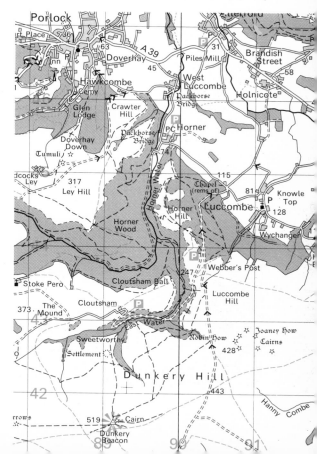

These paths are listed as H2 and H3 in the booklets *Waymarked Walks 1, 2* and *3* published by the Exmoor National Park Authority – they are actually described in booklet 2, which was not available. The $2\frac{1}{2}$-inch-to-the-mile maps in the booklets do not show contours and I thought the trio rather confusing and expensive. The National Park Centre is at Dulverton and there are information offices at Minehead, at County Gate (on the A39 between Lynmouth and Porlock), Lynmouth Parish Hall and Combe Martin. The last three are seasonal. Leaflets are available for nature trails on North Hill, Minehead and at Cloutsham.

Croydon Hill (Brendon Forest)

973 420, picnic place, forest roads, FC
This pleasant acre, a clearing in the pines, is reached via Dunster village (touristy but tasteful). Turn left towards Luxborough from the A396 Tiverton road about a mile south-west of Dunster. There are no Forestry Commission walks arranged – indeed there were preparations for a motor rally when I visited – but it is not difficult to keep your bearings in the hilly country. A waymarked walk surfaces here – 'D2' to Timberscombe.

Two other Forestry Commission picnic places are on the unclassified road from Wheddon Cross to Raleigh's Cross – at Kennisham, *963 359*, and Chargot, *965 355*.

Wootton Courtenay is a centre for walks in the coniferized commons which lie to the north and east.

Driving to Exmoor
Minehead describes itself as the Gateway to Exmoor. There are fine palm trees in the public park, a variety of restaurants and plenty of back-street parking, usually under whitebeams of the hybrid between *Sorbus aria* and *S. aucuparia*, the leaf amusingly indecisive between lobes or leaflets. There are walks on North Hill and in the (private) woods of Conygar.

To drive to Exmoor I would recommend Dulverton as the 'gateway', avoiding the busy, narrow coastal road. The Exe Valley is largely coniferized, in places impressive with old spruces and Douglas firs, but there are thick oakwoods in the Barle Valley. You can choose this route to Winsford Hill and South Hill, north of Dulverton, National Trust lands preserving 1100 acres of moorland here heavily invaded by thorns, presumably because they are not overgrazed. Such signs of returning woodland are profoundly interesting – and the hawthorns will be spectacular in late May. Winsford village, with its simple church and wooded hill, is charming. The Exmoor foothills about **Withypool Common** are remarkable for the many fine beech hedges, which are properly maintained, being essential windbreaks. They can be seen in all stages of growth. The distinctive, graceful yet grotesque patterns of old beech hedges are typical of Somerset hill farms. They seem to grow very vigorously, exposed on the tops of ancient hedge banks. There is no machine to keep the hedges in shape; only human skill can do it. The effect is worth our attention.

Croydon Hill, the forest road

Beech hedges near Withypool

South-East Devon and the Quantocks Landranger sheets 181, 193

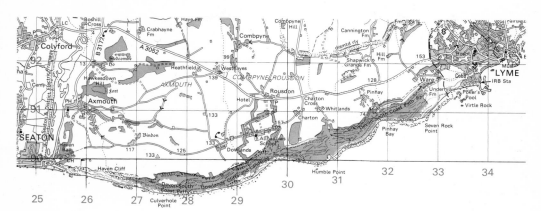

Lyme Regis to Axmouth Undercliff

327 915 to 254 902, ♀, 5½m hard going each way, NNR

This famous nature reserve was discovered by Professor Tansley. The Dowlands Landslip in 1839 opened a chasm, which has been filled by natural ashwood and native jungle: this is in the western half. In the eastern part (east of a beech-filled coombe or chine at Charton) there is more of the same, but here you can sit under an oak tree and look at the sea, while inhaling the scent of wild garlic. In the western half you see no oaks, and you march through a fantastic landscape: columns of ivy about the tall ashes, hanging lianas of *Clematis* and an impenetrable underbush where elder, bramble and ivy compete for every inch of space; even so there is room for primroses and wood spurge. The effect of this extraordinarily exuberant vegetation against the tall sugar-loaf shapes of the chalk cliffs is unforgettable.

Landslips reveal new ground, so the woodland could be described as uniquely primary, or at least 'natural secondary'. The growth of ivy is staggering. Having reached the top of a tree it continues to grow in long hanging fronds – against its nature, downwards. Usually this plant has no place in native woodland – this is the exception to the rule, a result of the frost-free air, the shelter and the strong light from the sea. Ivy makes

Chalk cliffs in the Lyme Regis landslip

Tree-clad ramparts of Neroche Castle

most of its growth before the late-leafing ash.

There are nicely rounded holm oaks in the central part, rowan and birch in the more acid, sandy eastern half. Madder and stinking iris grow here, and no doubt many other plants I did not notice in primrose time. There are large hart's tongue ferns everywhere, and much cuckoo pint. A leaflet may be available at Lyme. There is no access apart from Barn Close Lane, Seaton at the west, and the Ware Cliffs at the east. The path is part of the Devon South Coast Path.

There is another landslip at the **Spittles**, below Timber Hill, Lyme Regis, with a tiny parking place at *344 932*. This area is largely meadow with old hedges: 130 acres National Trust, leased to the Royal Society for Nature Conservancy. The woodland is scrub in the dangerous unstable part. Timber Hill has fine tall beeches with unsuitable *Tsuga* understorey: perhaps young beeches will be

planted or encouraged: the *Tsugas* will shelter them.

The Forestry Commission woodlands inland are of little interest. **St Marys Forest**, Trinity Hill, *305 955*, has a filthy parking place but a pleasant perimeter bridleway with ancient hedge trees including Scots pine. The forest itself is not open. Wootton Hill, called **Charmouth Forest**, is open. You can drive in at various points: *355 975* is one. The plantation is mature. It is quiet and dark, most of the available light being efficiently absorbed into production of softwood timber.

Neroche Forest *274 157*, ♀, *2200 acres, forest trail, 2½m or 1½m, mud, FC*
The eleventh-century castle ramparts are set with 150-year-old oaks, beeches, chestnuts and larches. Castle Farm, in the ramparts, is 200 years old and has a respectably foul midden. Water is pumped from half way up the hill,

where greensand outcrops over clay and limestone. The bare hilltop of the castle commands views of Wales on clear days – when I was there a mist concentrated attention on the more immediate view, which is suitably poetical. The trail takes you in a rough arc through the Castle Plantations below, where, somehow, you are conscious of being in the remains of a mediaeval forest even though the forestry is modern. The oldest trees are Japanese larch, planted in 1940 and now about 70 feet high. These are at point 7 of the trail, west of the castle. The trail includes several important forestry species, including Lawson cypress, and the attractively produced leaflet, available on site, identifies the trees as you go.

There is another access point at *229 164*, a picnic place in the old Prior's Park, 6 miles south of Taunton.

The ridged and beautiful countryside between the Axe and the Exe has many woods and will repay more detailed exploration than is possible in a countrywide survey. An immediate introduction is to be found at **Farway** Countryside Park, *187 942*, which has woodland as well as ponies and farm animals.

Looking east from East Hill Strips

An outer rampart of the Forestry Commission's Neroche Forest is at the interesting long-ridge woodland of **East Hill**, with ample parking space at *117 930* and elsewhere provided by Devon County Council. East Hill Strips are parallel wood-banks forty paces apart with extremely picturesque old polled and hedged beeches. There is a longish

walk here – the ridge is 3 miles long – but the motor road runs alongside. Could this ridge really have been an old boundary of the Neroche Forest, centred over 12 miles away?

A more complex escarpment carries a small wood on **Sheldon Hill** *114 093* above South Farm. This belongs to the Woodland Trust. Like many other Woodland Trust properties it does not offer much of a walk, and it is at present rather messily coniferized, though much of the ancient character of the margins remains – the ridge lanes provide the walking. It must be said that the Woodland Trust is the only organization working against the enormous loss of native woodland which has occurred in the last forty years. In time this pioneering work will be gratefully appreciated, and volunteers will flock to assist in management and restoration.

THE QUANTOCKS

Leaving the motorway (M5) at junction 24 between Bridgwater and Taunton avoids traffic delays and brings you at once into the steep, hedged lanes where perspective seems to be on holiday. The hedges are all sheared mechanically, which contours them smoothly to the roads and of course is death to any aspiring hedgerow tree, but vigorous growth here keeps the hedges thick.

Fyne Court, *223 321*, in the tiny village of Broomfield, west of North Petherton, has a Visitors' Centre which is nearly always open. Several woodland walks and a nature trail start here and there are painted interpretation panels for wet days. The beautiful parkland is full of scraps of old woodland, some 'promoted' from old coppices.

Quantock Forest *190 363 (Cockercombe Camp* ♀ ♣*), 168 377 (Rams Combe* ♣*), various walks, FC*
The main Forestry Commission parking ground takes you into what seems a corner of Oregon, in spite of the British flag flying at the Scripture Society's permanent camp. The tall, alien conifers are very impressive, but are, I believe, an outrage on the curvaceous

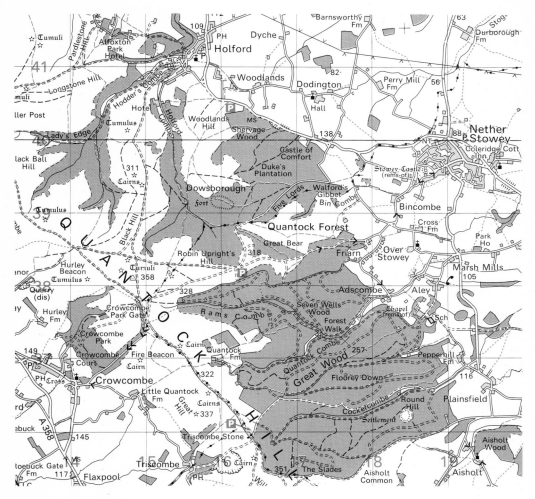

intimacies of the Quantock coombes. Getting to this part involves you with Nether Stowey and the busy A39: not worth it for Coleridge's dull cottage.

By contrast the Cockercombe viewpoint is very quiet. Spruce, hemlock and larch fill the valley, but the carefully arranged Disabled Viewpoint could make someone's day, and the approaches, with fine boundary beeches, are superb. The bridleway along the south side of the forest offers a recommendable walk with Aisholt Common open on your left. Then, striking right into the forest, it is not difficult to follow the larch-filled coombe downwards and back to the Camp (it is a prehistoric one).

A road through the trees runs parallel to Cockercombe on its north side.

Two National Trust woodland-and-heath sites are reached from the A39. **Shervage Wood**, 136 acres of oak, with coppice, has a parking place at *161 404*. Don't leave valuables in the car. Longstone Hill, 61 acres, is reached via **Hodder's Combe** and the village of Holford, a short detour from the main road. The land is heath, but the way lies through ragged old beeches; silver-grey bark with the blue greys of sea and sky, the dark pink of the rock, and paintbox-green moss. Park by the ancient dogpen, *153 412*.

The Somerset, Dorset and Wiltshire Borders Landranger sheets 183, 184, 194, 195

Alfred's Tower

A clear landmark to be seen from the north and west is Alfred's Tower, *745 351*, a sturdy folly on a rather logical triangular plan, erected by Henry Hoare the 2nd, of Stourhead, to commemorate Alfred's victory over the Danes eleven centuries before – as good a reason as any for building a folly. The hill on which it stands is 770 feet high. Lines of beeches, very picturesque and sprawling by the narrow approach road almost constitute a wood, and provide a long glade to park in, apart from the National Trust car park for the tower itself. Bridleways into the ridge-top woodland do not seem to lead very far before dipping to the plain, but it is easy enough to find a roughly oval or a floppy orbital route around the tower, through spruce woods planted amongst old beeches. Old or new, all the trunks are vividly modelled by lichen in green and black. You can also walk through to the Stourhead Estate, about 2 miles south-eastwards.

Downhill and westwards is the little town of Bruton, heavy with charm, which gives its name to the Bruton Forest. Only scattered woods remain of this forest, which has no particular history; 1000 acres belong to the Forestry Commission. Many elms survive by the B3092 south from Frome. The elm is a farmland tree, but something of the forest atmosphere survives around Gare Hill – and many forest names.

Great Bradley Wood and Gare Hill

797 404, ♀ ♠, *2½m walk, pf*
Between the great houses and parks of Longleat and Stourhead lies a broad sheaf of fine woodland mostly on greensand ridges. At the map reference you can just park one car in the farm road, and follow a clearly signed footpath under elms with a rhododendron understorey into a splendid plantation, a wonderful blend of forestry and landscape design. Large areas are being cleared of underwood, revealing the trunks of excellent oaks, and well-grown conifers line the route:

grand fir, Douglas fir, Sawara cypress, Sitka spruce. You are warned not to leave the pathway, but there really is no need. Bear left to reach an exit at a picturesque corner with old beeches, or right to Gare Hill village.

Stourhead *779 349*, ♀ ♠, *2507 acres, 1½m lakeside walk, NT*

The pleasure gardens, begun in 1741, surround an artificial lake below the tastefully preserved village of Stourton. There is a hotel, with parking for patrons, but definitely nowhere to park in the village. The National Trust car park is above on the hilltop. You must choose, and turn aside from the gateway of the house (except for a look at the mighty sweet chestnuts by the drive) if you want to spend your time with the trees: or allow time for the house and its treasures as well.

Magic is a word which enters all but the barest description of Stourhead, and it is a sort of double enchantment. First was the idea (of Henry Hoare, the banker's son) to build classical temples in a landscape designed to be 'natural' – rejecting the then traditional formality of gardens. Second is the enchantment that has settled over the beautiful valley, which is now filled with well-grown conifers planted by the Victorian Hoares: conservation has waved a wand and the whole thing looks perfect. A vulgar mediaeval cross – a gift from Bristol where it was much disliked in the 1750s – fits in as well as, in the parkland above, an obelisk with a zany face on top. Down by the water are the tallest Macedonian pines in Britain (a graceful five-needle pine with pale green shoots) and the tallest noble firs in England, with fine *Thuja plicata* and the biggest tulip trees in Britain. These will not last forever, but the National Trust has carefully planted new ones. All are sheltered and kept in visual proportion by the high valley sides of the prosaically named Six Wells Bottom, once a bleak place where the headwaters of the Stour gathered in pools.

The pretty temples accurately absorb the

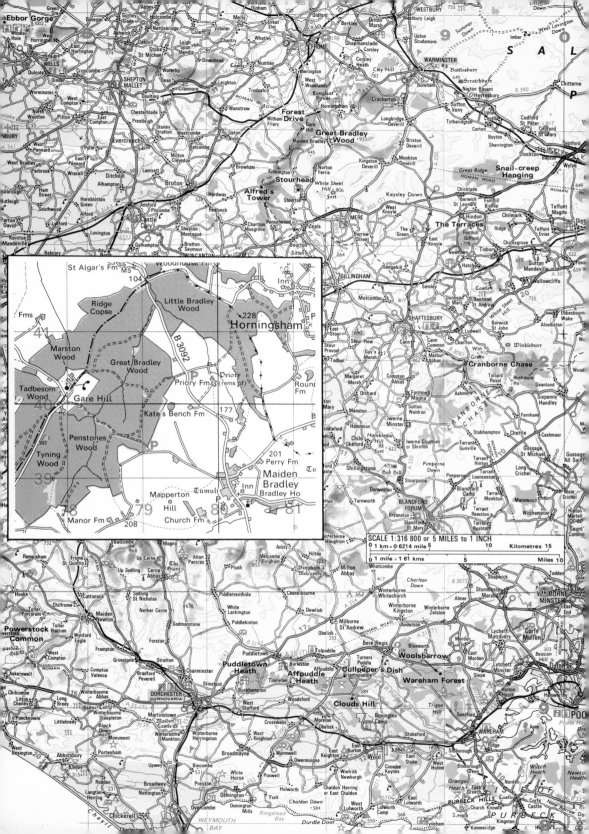

Stourhead

Forest Drive from Maiden Bradley to Horningsham

Keeping left at junctions, minor roads skirt the woodlands and have wide grassy verges inviting a stop: there are short walks in the trees. At the Bath Arms above Horningsham are tables under strange little lopped limes. From here the road to Warminster goes straight through the conifer woodlands of Longleat, with many metalled forest roads open to exploration.

Beyond Warminster is the mightier country of the chalk downs.

Snail-creep Hanging *955 365,* ♀, *fps, pf*

Take the No Through Road from the railway bridge east of Sherrington and drive as far as possible. The Snail-creep glistens ahead, a chalk track, at first through bleached grass, elders and hawthorns. Continuing uphill there are wayfaring trees and sloes, buckthorn, bramble, privet, rose, then scrubby birch, beech and oak. The path divides into several, roughly parallel ones, in the manner of the old chalk pathways – avoiding obstacles long since

last rays of the sun, while the elegant firs, spruces and *Sequoiadendron* are delicately outlined against the shadows; beeches, more translucent, flame dramatically. The lake is a place to linger until the last light gleams. All this thanks to the Hoares' possessing both money and taste.

The path to Snail-creep Hanging, looking towards Salisbury Plain

vanished. Juniper and whitebeam appear, holly and hazel hint at real woodland, but the gleaming trunks of ashes, with some planted spruce beyond, suggest that this was once grassland. Beech and fine, tall whitebeams fill grassy spaces where burdock thrives. Near the top of the down the chalk disappears below sand. Snail-creep Hanging is not a beech hanger but an old hazel and oak coppice, now well organized for shooting. You have been walking south: presently a straight ride, in fact an old Roman road, goes right and west along the ridge, spruce forestry on the left, oak woodland on the right. You can continue for 2 miles or so, or turn north when a convenient track appears, and back to rejoin one of the downward valley trackways which converge eastwards on to Sherrington Down. You'd never guess at all this richness below you as you sweep by on the A303(T).

South of this main road is Fonthill Bishop, where the public highway goes through the park gates and by the ornamental lake. Through Fonthill Gifford you reach the mighty beeches of **The Terraces**, *917 322*, where there is a ridgeway track. But Fonthill itself, the colossal abbey built for £300,000 in 1799 by the dilettante Beckford – the site now marked by very tall conifers – is private. Not long ago all was open and you could thread your way by a fallen *Araucaria* and a mighty redwood to mouldering garden nymphs and the weedy steps of the misbegotten structure – it was felled by the wrath of a storm almost before it was finished. There is a footpath through some of the very tall beech and spruce woods from Beacon Hill; *912 217*.

Sixpenny Handley, *990 180*, and Tollard Royal are centres for Cranborne Chase, which contains a long strip of woodland. Chases were subject to forest laws but privately owned – this one since James I. Owners and their keepers were often at war with poachers and others asserting what they believed to be their rights. Weapons are preserved at Farnham Museum. The woods of Cranborne Chase remain well guarded old coppices, now mainly coniferized, though chase laws were abolished in the early nineteenth century.

DORSET HEATHS

Large forests occupy the Dorset heathlands east of Dorchester, an area rich in tree interest though one may deeply regret the loss of heathland habitat. The large **Wareham Forest** is traversed by a long straight road north-west from Wareham to Bere Regis. Here, $1\frac{1}{2}$ miles from Wareham, one may park and follow a forest trail which passes a bog nature reserve and a small arboretum. The pines are as dull as can be, on ground deeply ridged by the plough, and pylons litter the skylines. There is a smart campsite, the Wareham Forest Tourist Centre, with a good children's play area, further along the road, and farms sell local produce, including cream. The ancient fortified hilltop of **Woolsbarrow**, *892 925*, is a 19-acre heathland nature reserve reached by forest rides from the A35 or from the road through the forest. The plantation is large and you will need two Ordnance Survey maps (sheets 194 and 195) and, if the sky is overcast, a compass.

Isolated fragments of preserved heathland are, I feel, a poor substitute for the real thing, vast and various, and most interesting where wetlands or woodlands merge. At **Clouds Hill**, *824 909*, just south of Lawrence of Arabia's Cottage (National Trust and smothered in rhododendron), you may see what the Army tanks do to the heath. There is even a small car park provided. Considering that the Army also preserves large patches from its own infernal machines one may conclude that the Forestry Commission is the more destructive, ploughing and then blanketing the ground with dense conifer crops, so that the native gorse, heather and grasses and their attendant fauna are lost for ever. Driving towards Dorchester by minor roads from Clouds Hill you can divert north-west to Tolpuddle and cheer yourself up with the Martyrs' Tree, an ancient, propped-up sycamore preserved by the T.U.C. There are useful parking places which allow access to remnants of heathland vegetation: at **Cullpepers Dish**, *815 925*, and **Affpuddle Heath**, *804 925*. **Puddletown Heath**, with Hardy's birthplace at *728 924*, is heavily coniferized,

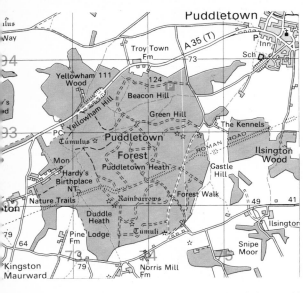

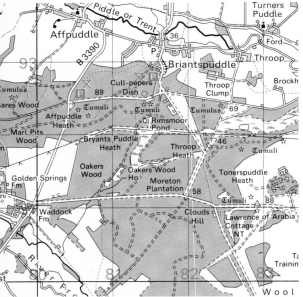

West of Dorchester, fork right $4\frac{1}{2}$ miles out of the town on to a ridge (Roman) road, the A35(T), over the vivid scenery of tumuli-studded downs to Powerstock Common.

Powerstock Common *547 974, ♀, 4m or less, easy, 100 acres, NR (and FC)*
You can no longer book a railway ticket to Toller Porcorum, but you can walk along the suture of the railway which is stitched with a pretty vegetation inadequately described as scrub. Blackthorn, field rose and wayfaring tree grow on the chalky embankment above a placid stream. Healthy young oak trees invade, and lovely old goat willows remember the days of steam.

A mile west of Toller the railway crossed a lane by a bridge, which remains, and its line continues as the north-west boundary of the nature reserve. Here, at the map reference, is a small parking place. The nature reserve land is interlocked with Forestry Commission plantations of pines and *Tsuga*, seemingly threatened by the forestry but in fact protected, for it is doubtful if these 100 acres would have survived without the help of the Commission. The bridleway leads you to a wood-bank with a line of bent oaks where ash and hazel are coppiced to make a grove to delight the eye. What appears to have been a line of ancient fishponds leads to a patch of heather, gorse and rushes, and more old oak-crowned banks ten paces apart provide a corridor of natural vegetation to the south-east part of the reserve, where bracken heath declines to woodland of oak and willow. It is all beautiful and remote, and the setting of sculptured hills is the more impressive for the lines of conifers which accentuate the curving skyline.

Ebbor Gorge *525 485, 2m, steep, 142 acres, NT (NR)*
Park at the Churchill Memorial $1\frac{1}{2}$ miles from Wells, 2 miles south of Wookey Hole. The limestone gorge contains a rich ash-oak wood. A fine polished axe found in a cave at the head of the gorge is now in Wells Museum. There are good views from the top and from the cliffs of the gorge.

with rhododendron and cherry laurel to boot, but a (rather dirty) parking place at *743 936* is approached via handsome beeches on a south-facing outcrop of chalk, where even the fastidious may be tempted to stop. There is no need yet to join the A35(T): the minor road runs on via Stinsford, where Hardy's heart is buried and sheltered by nice trees.

Salisbury and the New Forest

Landranger sheets 183, 184, 195, 196

WEST AND EAST OF SALISBURY

Wilton Park, in the old town of Wilton, has fine cedars, hemlocks, planes and flowering cherries, and a selection of exotic specimen broadleaves; but there are many better and larger arboreta. A beech-lined road south-west (signposted Broad Chalke) leads to the Forestry Commission coniferized woods of **Hare Warren**, *081 288*. You can drive along the lanes west and east, and especially to the west on Hunt's Down, and walk along well-surfaced paths – many do, for woods are scarce here. There is a lot of rubbish but a good view; beeches, birches, gorse and blackthorn at the margins.

Great Yews, *120 230*, and **Little Yews** are woods south of Homington, which is east of Coombe Bissett, across the A354.

Grovely Wood West *015 349*, ↟, *about 2000 acres, easy, FC*

Grovely Wood was once an oakwood in the more acid soils held on top of a limestone ridge. Access is from the minor road between Dinton and Wylye. Near the crest of the downs, turn eastwards down a track for about a mile. The eastern end is controlled by the Wilton Park Estate; fine, large beeches on the slopes with ash thrusting in at clearings. In the Forestry Commission's western part the old character has gone, and a great crop of larch nursed by beech is now perhaps ten years old. There being nothing much to see, I read the Forestry Commission bylaws: you can take a pushchair provided there is an infant in it, but no other vehicle.

Birch, ash, oak, and sallow are springing at the margins; depressed wood spurge and wan-

Sunlight and shadow on the young forest of Grovely Wood

flowered primroses remain under some Douglas firs – not for long. But, as I waited for a shower or two to pass, the place began to grow on me: it is silent, high, lonely and, after all, full of trees. Watching the clouds and their shadows form a wooden 'high seat', I decided it was beautiful.

A WOODLAND DRIVE, EAST FROM SALISBURY

Alderbury *185 273*
Mainly through private coniferized woodlands this includes many aspects of original woodland trees and hedges, particularly beeches, yews, some coppiced hazel, and many characterful oaks. Take the road out of Alderbury to Farley, across the A36(T) by the bridge. Farley's streets form a rough oval – leave by the opposite side signposted Winterslow. At the junction of the East Grimstead to Winterslow road a farm road used as a public footpath leads across the Forestry Commission's **Bentley Wood**, a 2-mile walk to West Tytherley. Cars must go more circuitously to West Tytherley via East Grimstead and West Dean, but will pass a strange old oak near the site of a Roman villa in the Dun Valley. At *234 288* is the 72-acre **Blackmoor Copse**, a nature reserve with coppiced hazel, habitat for white and purple emperors and silver-washed fritillary. From West to East Tytherley is comparatively woodless: then continue south to Lockerley, and turn left to Mottisfont on the B3084 going north. For 3 miles this road runs through open oakwoods with beech. Turn sharp right before Broughton: on the hilltop is a really lovely parking place, where someone has planted daffodils under a line of old beeches. The view is over the Wallop Brook to Danebury Down. You are on a Roman road (Winchester to Old Sarum).

Harewood Forest *404 441*, ♀(♠),
1900 acres, about 1 hour or all day,
many easy paths and rides, pf
Secretive and from outside plain-looking, with no special parking places and no notices, welcoming or otherwise, Harewood lies on its

TOP: the view over the Wallop Brook, from *317 312*
ABOVE: charcoal burning in Harewood Forest

hill above the Test, breathing gently like a dragon unslain. His old fangs are mossy oaks and birches with double and treble stems; his rotting molars ancient stubs of oak – acres of them. Clouds of real, not imaginary smoke emerge from his belly, for charcoal is made here. The burners are cauldron-shaped with pipes at odd angles, set amongst the sessile oak standards in a space the size of a football ground. Already the ground cleared last year is planted with new oaks. There are large stands of larch fenced from the deer, which are many. I did not see any hares, and birds other than pheasants and woodpigeons seemed to be absent. The map reference gives a parking place on the A303(T), a noisome and noisy spot. Cleared underwood and probably, still, charcoal burning, are towards Cow Down at the west side. There are several points of entry; only Upping Copse to the tail-end, south-west, seems to be private. I could not explore the whole forest: I hope you can. Take a compass if the day is dull, and plot your route on a bit of paper.

THE NEW FOREST

♀ ♣ ♨, *105 sq m, FC*

Nearly half of these 67,082 acres, administered by the Forestry Commission, is woodland, with one-third of this unenclosed, 'natural', woodland often the remains of old inclosures. The rest is open heath, bog and grassland with scattered trees and small woods. The National Forest Park is 40 square miles larger than the forest, and includes some, though not all, of a series of contiguous commons totalling 6299 acres to the north and west, and some farmland towards the coast at the south. Some of the commons belong to the National Trust, and join imperceptibly to the forest heaths, beasts being allowed to wander indiscriminately. In fact the forest itself is a large common, or a mosaic of common land with the inclosures for timber belonging to the Crown. Within the forest are large areas of private land, as well as towns, villages, roads, farms, riding schools and many hotels. The Forestry Commission

Ageing beech in Tantany Wood, home of Sika deer, where oaks, beeches and thorns flourish and die untouched. Westwards, interrupted only by the railway, is the largest area of continuous woodland in the New Forest. Park at Culverley, *367 047*, among pines and birches.

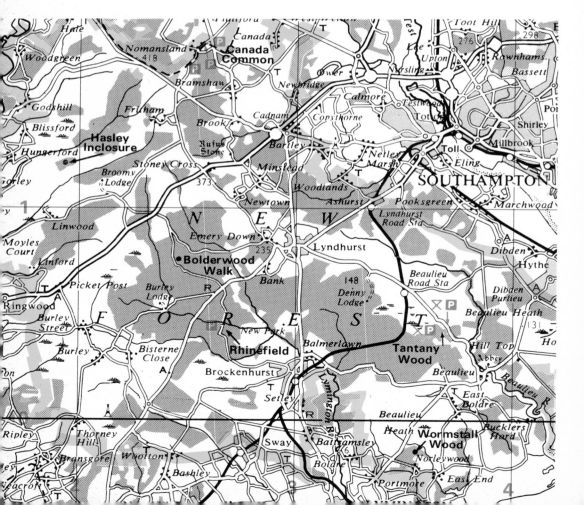

Canada Common, National Trust, *287 172*, adjoins Furzley and Cadnam at the north of the New Forest. Beyond the heath are trees on every horizon, while houses, beasts – and people collecting wood or just walking – give a domestic atmosphere.

maintains 130 parking grounds, most with picnic places, and several camping grounds. Of 129 wooded 'inclosures', thirty are ancient woods now unenclosed.

The Forestry Commission has to work alongside the Court of Verderers (which looks after the needs of the commoners who graze 5000 animals in the forest) and its duty is to conserve the 'Ancient and Ornamental' woodlands, to keep the balance between conifer and broadleaf with a minimum of disturbance to the latter, and to maintain the two Ornamental Drives of exotic trees. The Nature Conservancy is consulted, and drainage of bogs is allowed only where it is necessary to preserve the woodlands. The commoners' horses and cattle conserve the heathland naturally apart from some 'rehabilitation' (burning). Where new trees do spring up they remain unenclosed.

The Hampshire Basin, facing south and for many centuries of the post-glacial period connected by land to the continent of Europe, was a sort of natural tree nursery in prehistoric time. Species now native to Scotland here survived the last of the Ice Ages, and as the ice retreated northwards, but before the sea rose to form the English Channel, oaks, elms, beeches and limes took root here as the European forest spread back to the British peninsula.

Near the middle of the Basin a segment of impermeable rock covered by sand, gravel and clay forms a series of plateaux intersected by shallow stream valleys. Because of the hard rock below, the lower ground, and some of the higher, is ill-drained, and heath turns to bog. But, partly because of the benign climate,

Massive trunk of Douglas fir, one of a group by Black Water stream at the south end of Tall Trees walk, Rhinefield. Car park at *266 047* is well appointed and centre for several walks. Tallest tree is *Sequoiadendron*, 160 feet, about 300 yards north. Most were planted in 1859.

native trees regenerate freely, particularly the Scots pine. Before it was called a New Forest (in 1079 by William I) it was partly the waste of 45 manors named in Domesday, partly the property of the Saxon Kings, and partly common land since time immemorial. In fact ever since the Bronze Age when Jutish settlers on the coast and rivers grazed their animals on the heath, it can have changed comparatively little.

Before Neolithic times it was woodland of oak, beech, pine and perhaps lime. The first farmers cleared or killed the trees, grew crops for a few years, built burial mounds, then left the infertile soil once the woodland humus was exhausted. The land became heathy and the animals kept it so. It has miraculously survived for 1500 years, the largest area of unenclosed land in England.

The miracle has occurred because of the subtle balance between the rights of the commoners and the demands of the Crown, at first for the products of the chase, later for timber. Inclosures for whatever purpose could only be made provided sufficient land was left free for pasture and for a variety of other rights including commons of mast (pigs to eat nuts and acorns for 60 days), turbary ($\frac{1}{3}$ of turf cut for domestic fuel), estovers, or fuel wood, also domestic only, and marl, from twenty-three pits for manure. Only the right of pasture is now largely used.

While this beautiful balance of opposing demands has kept the forest intact, both demands have of course modified the vegetation very considerably. Deer and ponies, cattle and donkeys, all will eat hazel before they bother with gorse, while the Navy, from the seventeenth century to the nineteenth, demanded open-grown pedunculate oaks with copiously spreading branches to provide the crucks and knees for the ribs of ships. This is often pointed out, but did they not also need planks from straight-grown trees? Scots pines were first planted in 1776, at Ocknell Clump, and have since become the dominant tree of the forest, that is if you disregard gorse as being a bush.

The New Forest Act of 1870 largely perpetuated the nature, shape and picturesque character of the area. From the point of view of natural history its main interest is in its bogs, in its long-untended woodland, and in its relative size, which enables the survival of true heathland habitat.

But many new threats have occurred in the last hundred years: some, like a couple of airfields, have been absorbed, even turned to recreational use. Only forty years ago there was much argument over whether the main roads should be fenced, thus destroying the continuity of heaths and woods. Now the forest is neatly sliced in three by the A31(T) and A35, and further fragmented by the A337 running north to south. The skyline is everywhere sawn

Beaulieu Heath. Gorse grows high and spreads very widely on old runways of Hatchet Moor airfield – part of a remarkable unbroken tract of heath, at least 4 square miles. Large parking place (and model aeroplane field) at *348 006* – and several others on the heath.

In extreme contrast yet adjacent to the heath is the ancient Wormstall Wood: oak, holly, some pine, blackthorn and bog myrtle (above) by Crockford Stream. Park at Norley Inclosure, *346 982*, and walk east through spruce plantation.

and pierced by the outline of alien conifers – and by shining industrial smoke stacks to the east. The fame of the forest, its ponies and its posh pubs brings 7 million visitors a year, who deposit 2000 tons of litter, not all of it successfully removed by the patient foresters. Tons of yellow gravel are deposited to make car parks and forest roads. A thick ring of new houses surrounds the perimeter. Planes and helicopters cross the northern half every few minutes. In spite of all this the forest remains at peace, enwrapped in its own unique atmosphere.

The New Forest is a national institution and everyone is entitled to have ideas about its use and preservation. The Forestry Commission is doing a wonderful job, but I think its terms of reference should be revised. The statutory timber inclosures were increased to 5000 acres as recently as 1949. Perhaps a forest should always produce timber, but there should be no need for alien conifers here, particularly as the Scots pine grows so well. The system of statutory inclosure should be revised in the light of pure conservation and all should be cleared of alien conifers as the crops mature, and returned to natural vegetation, at first enclosed from grazing. Although the Commission's conservation control is essential, notices should be removed or reduced and less raucously yellow gravel obtained (the Commission claims it is local, and they would use no other), forest roads being destroyed once finished with. Private land should be bought in when it becomes available. Features like Rhinefield House, recently sold, should be preserved. The place needs museums. The present Ornamental Drives form the nucleus of a fine arboretum and new specimen trees ought to be planted instead of the surrounding blocks of timber trees. The overgrown rhododendrons should be removed. This area, South Bolderwood and North Rhinefield, forms a natural focus for visitors.

As a National Forest Park under heavy pressure the forest deserves not to be flown over below 2000 feet, and not to be used as a short cut for heavy lorries. The main roads should be routed around or tunnelled under. Eventually perhaps cars should be banned, an underground railway being substituted – in the meantime there ought to be an enforced speed limit of 20 mph. The Forestry Commission should keep pigs if no commoners will.

A former deputy surveyor described the New Forest as a 'pre-Norman landscape'. Let us keep it so.

The forest is divided into 'walks', old administrative areas like parishes in a town, and these fifteen regions make a good basis for exploring the forest; they are used in the official guidebook. With 129 large woods to choose from I cannot be any sort of guide.

Little Witch and Great Witch, small hills near Hasley Inclosure. Pine regenerates easily over heathland remote from traffic and only lightly grazed. Footpath east from Ogdens, *182 124*, over Latchmore Brook. Approach via South Gorley.

Trying to be systematic, I have investigated the six or so different types of countryside in the forest. In such a forest park I think one must regard all the different types of country as potentially interesting – perhaps potentially woodland.

A leaflet map comes from the Forestry Commission, Queen's House, Lyndhurst.

The official guide, *Explore the New Forest*, is excellent, with detailed walkers' maps, interesting articles illustrated in colour, useful addresses, book list, etc. HMSO.

Major Forestry Commission walks with leaflets are Bolderwood Walk, Ornamental Drive (Rhinefield), Oberwater Walk. The Rhinefield Ornamental Drive leaflet is essential.

Ringwood Forest, to the west of the New Forest, is heavily coniferized and not generally open to walkers. It provides a pleasant drive. In the larger context of the Forestry Commission's Ringwood Forest are picnic places, with walks, at **Broom Hill**, *050 035*,

(turn south from the Three Legged Cross to Holt road), and, close to Bournemouth – $\frac{1}{2}$ mile east of Hurn – the Rams Down car park by the Avon. Near Ringwood itself, 2 miles south-west, is the **Avon Forest Country Park**, with heath and pines, run by the Dorset County Council.

The Isle of Wight

Landranger sheet 196

Osborne *around 525 952,* ♀ ♣, *1m, muddy, Crown property*

The woods begin only a mile from the East Cowes Ferry, or you can start the walk from the Swiss Cottage in the grounds of Osborne House. Parking is available here between April and September. Queen Victoria's Swiss Cottage was designed to have a view of the sea, and the view is still there between the trees. A dark green gate to your right leads to a fairy-tale woodland by the shore. Turn left downhill for *Cupressus macrocarpa* and *Pinus radiata*, the latter truly magnificent and threatening to burst a circular iron seat built long ago round its base. There are also some very old and characterful oaks which, though less in stature than the largest of the *macrocarpa*, must date back to before 1844, when Albert designed the great house for his Queen. In fact there are many suggestions of old woodland amongst the exotic trees: durmast oak, wood sage beneath the redwoods, butcher's broom under the *Ilex* on the shore; and primroses in the mud of the paths. In spite of the great size and vigour of the pines, evergreen oaks and cypresses, it is the redwoods which give these woods their strange atmosphere. They are quite naturalized and, over bright green moss, form a true wilderness, with the rotting trunks of other trees including many silver birches. The coast redwood, *Sequoia sempervirens*, the only species of the genus remaining from the family Taxodiaceae, formed a worldwide forest in the Cretaceous: fossils of the trees a hundred million years old are found in the rocks of the Isle of Wight, as they are in the American Yellowstone.

It was absolutely quiet in the wood, except for the gentle lapping of the Solent and a distant sound of bells. Surveyors were at work, and there may be plans, no doubt long overdue, to humanize this wilderness. The woods terminate vaguely at the south-east on private land and it is best to return roughly the way you came to avoid a long and boring walk back by road.

Brighstone Forest *419 846,* ♀ ♣, *at least 2 walks of up to 4m total, rough in places, NT, FC*

The parking place is for the National Trust, which is much in evidence on the downs, but the woods are in the control of the Forestry Commission. Turn off the B3401 Newport to Freshwater road to Calbourne. This is countryside for hikers and ramblers prepared to be energetic. The forest lies just off the chalk and is planted with now nearly mature Corsican pine, but there is beech as well. In fact, the woods are everywhere penetrated by beech, the natural dominant – deposed but continuing a sort of guerilla resistance.

Following part of the Tennyson Trail along the ridge eastwards from the car park takes you uphill for $\frac{3}{4}$ mile along the edge of the forest, then, on the level, follow the signposted Worsley Trail for a few yards past a covered reservoir, where turkey oaks and Monterey pines are planted. Then turn into the forest by the bridleway. Downhill and bearing right you will soon see a wooden gate which leads to a hedge along the forest margin. The hedge is worth seeing: oak, hazel and hawthorn weirdly shaped and intermingled. The true nature of the forest reveals itself – not regimented pines but a loose mixture of beech and hemlock with many ferns. The footpath continues across part of the down grassland, and into the trees again on Rowborough Down – the walk may be any length: strike up through the trees to find a forest road and you can be sure that it will lead you back to base, for the plantation is comparatively narrow.

Going west from the car park takes you on the Forestry Commission's Jubilee Walk and on to the National Trust downland above Mottistone. Here the woods sweep down to the Manor grounds and are well known for bluebells in May.

Brighstone Down is part of the chalk outcrop which divides the island east to west, though cut by the Medina River. The southern part contains the multifarious strata for which

The Osborne woodland walk, with large Monterey pine and circular seat

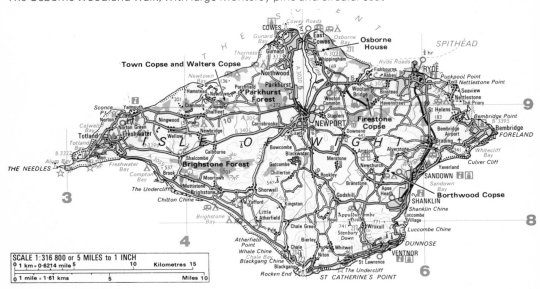

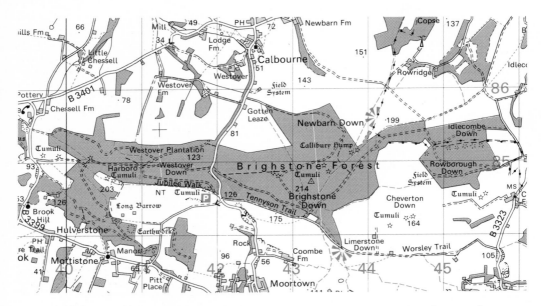

the Isle of Wight is famous; the northern part is clay, uninteresting for geologists but fine for oaks. All over the farmland the richly interlacing pattern of their branches and a peculiar compact rounded shape – perhaps this is a local subspecies of the English oak – beguile the eye and leave an impression of woodland where in fact there are only small groups of trees. Nevertheless, one does feel that the farmers are happy to have the trees about them. I saw several old oaks scattered about the fields where they would be in the way of modern machinery.

Newtown: Town Copse and Walters Copse 424 905, ♀ ♣, 100 acres, easy paths, NT

Fortunately some oakwood is preserved, and in the context of a beautiful, unspoilt corner of countryside at Newtown. The woods continue to the edge of the marshes – which are also a nature reserve. The Newtown Oyster Fishery Company occupies the Town Copse, and one cannot complain about this. The woods are visually uneventful but no doubt more interesting in summer than when I visited. Coppices are little more than thickets, but perhaps there are plans for regular coppicing. There are some taller oaks at the Town Copse side. Great elms were once a feature of Newtown, but they cannot have been indigenous and the sweetly simple and quiet village scene is now dominated by its own ancient town hall, against the always rich background of the oaks.

Parkhurst Forest 480 900, ♀ ♣, easy waymarked walks, 3½m or less, FC

I was expecting gloomy ranks of conifers surrounding the prison walls, but the place is cheerful enough, and well patronized. Some oakwood survives from planting after the Napoleonic Wars; the rest is fairly young coniferous plantation in the familiar Forestry Commission pattern with good gravelled roadways and a decent picnic place. Parkhurst is the largest wooded area in the island and is on the site of an old forest or chase.

There is another Forestry Commission picnic place in a beechwood at **Firestone Copse**, *559 911*, 2 miles west of Ryde, with a waymarked walk of 1½ miles including the Blackbridge Brook and two shorter walks. A National Trust wood of 57 acres near Sandown is **Borthwood Copse**, *573 846*.

The Robin Hill Country Park, *536 884*, looked absolutely awful, crudely commercial, and I didn't go in.

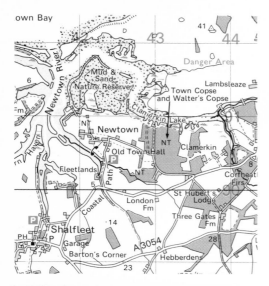

Richly embroidered stump of oak, Newtown

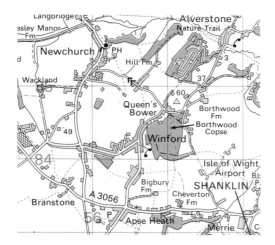

TOP: Wind-cut oak
ABOVE: *Cupressus macrocarpa*

SEASIDE TREES

Deciduous trees adapt to exposure by changing their shape. The oaks above are at Combe in north Devon.

Evergreens such as holm oak and tamarisk, lose their leaves in hard winters and recover slowly during the summer.

Two conifers well adapted to strong winds were introduced from California in the 1830s. The Monterey pine, *Pinus radiata*, has rugged bark and grows vigorously, often with heavy, sprawling limbs. The Monterey cypress, *Cupressus macrocarpa*, produces multiple, upward-thrusting branches and keeps its vaguely conical shape, growing tall and forming a heavy, buttress like bole. Both these retain their cones for many years.

Avon, the Mendips and Westonbir

Landranger sheets 172, 173, 182

BRISTOL

Leigh Woods *553 740 and 564 731,* ♀ ♣,
600 acres, various paths, FC, NT, NNR
The first map reference is for the Forestry
Commission's car park, reached by turning off
the A369, which runs roughly parallel to the
Avon Gorge. The second identifies the west
bank of the gorge at the Clifton Suspension
Bridge. From Bristol city centre simply make
for Clifton, cross the bridge on foot and turn
right, and you are on the Avon Walkway in the
National Trust-nature reserve part of the
woods. This is much the better part, with older
trees than at the Forestry Commission's
Stokeleigh Forest, to the west and north,
which has been degraded in the usual ways.
Coppice stumps remain amongst the birch and
ivy, and the coniferized sections are of very
little interest. But, of course, the car park is
very useful, and it is cosily placed well away
from the road. To get to the nature reserve,
leave the Forestry Commission's red and
yellow trails, striking off eastwards and turning
right at each opportunity until you reach the
reserve boundary, which has a signpost map.

The Avon woods are of oak, ash, beech and
yew, and also contain small-leaved lime. Three
very rare whitebeams grow on the cliffs of the
Gorge, two of them found nowhere else,
Sorbus bristoliensis and *S. wilmottiana*, while

the third, *S. anglica*, is more or less local to the
River Avon and the Mendips. The Avon
Gorge is of course wonderful scenery,
especially with Brunel's masterly addition, but
it is a shame that it must contain a busy motor
road. All the same, these are the wildest woods
you can expect to find anywhere so close to a
city.

Brockley Wood *484 664,* ♀ ♣, *nature trail,*
1m plus return, pf
Turn off the Bristol to Weston-super-Mare
road (A370) on to the minor road up Brockley
Combe (signposted Bristol Airport). The
nature trail is just a nice walk, marked with
posts carrying the initials NT, from a car park
near the top of the Combe. Yews among tall
oaks and beeches give an air of poetry and
mystery in spite of the rather rubbishy
roadside and the spruces crowded beyond the
fence.

Another footpath, from Cleeve, a mile south-west, traverses Goblin Combe. Turning right in Congresbury, which is another mile down towards Weston, brings you to a small road marked 'No right turn onto A370'. At this junction is a driveway marked as a footpath to **Cadbury Hill** (National Trust, 39½ acres including the Iron Age hill fort, *442 650*).

Cleeve, apparently somewhat suburban, has more than meets the eye: an atmosphere I cannot identify. It is of course an ancient home of man, yet nature seems to exert an unusual

force. I have never forgotten an evening walk here where, near some farm buildings, the air was thick with bats. The presence in the woods of spurge laurel reinforces my feeling – is there, I wonder, any correlation between the distribution of this weird plant and Iron Age dwellings?

Clevedon

For a look at the Levels, the wind-curved thorns and willows (some attractively pollarded), continue on the road past Cadbury

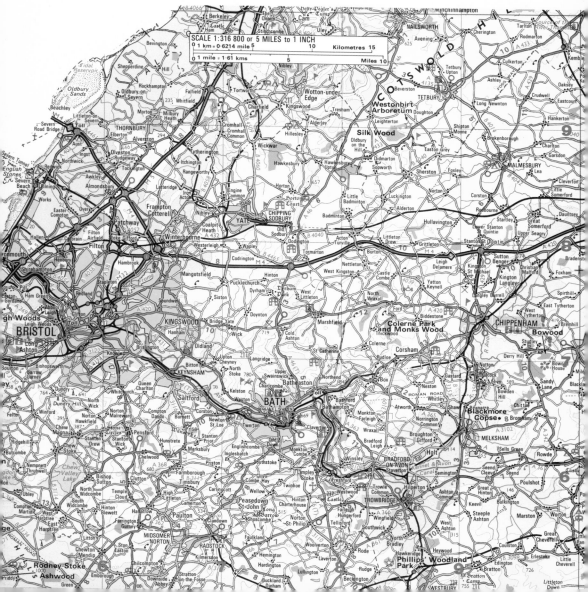

Wood pasture at Clevedon Warren

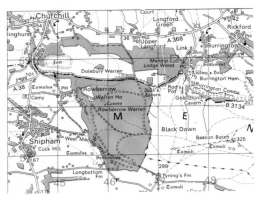

to Yatton and turn right after the railway bridge; continue thus over Kenn Moor to Clevedon Court (a National Trust manor house, with a chapel and terraced gardens, closed in winter) which has a magnificent plane tree and backs on to wooded hills familiar to travellers on the M5. These woods, described on the map as **The Warren**, *421 717*, are of very secondary character, but there are bridleways up the north slope, where there is a pig farm – trees standing in a sea of mud.

MENDIP WOODS

Rowberrow Woods *456 575 (Shipham)*, ♠, *650 acres, fp only, FC*
The well-marked lines of the hill fort remind us once again of the ancient history of the hills. Just the place for a few Austrian pines, thought

the Forestry Commission. You can walk through, but must stick to public rights-of-way; also, there is nowhere to park. You have to stop in School Lane, Shipham, and walk down to Rowberrow Bottom. Here you can join the Mendip Way going east.

Burrington Combe *476 587*, ♀ *(and yew)*, *fps*
The Combe is wooded, with almost pure ash/hazel on one side and quite large yews clinging to the rock slope on the other. There are several access points, all of which soon bring you out onto the Downs – but this is a better place than Cheddar Gorge for walkers interested in trees. A large parking place at the head of the Combe gives access to scrubland on the top.

Cheddar Gorge *482 545*, ♀, *318 acres, NT and nature trail, limited access, CNT*
The incredible commercialization of the caves stops suddenly, and wondering admiration takes over: one's driving becomes inaccurate. The National Trust part is around Black Rock, reached by a green gate where the road straightens out. On the dark, wet, December day of my visit I couldn't see very much, but the impression of golden ash trunks and black triangles of yews among the amazing rocks is distinct: a simple but satisfying pattern. It is also satisfying to realize that one of the more remarkable and famous parts of England can be preserved unspoilt.

    Cheddar Wood, *451 555*, on Callow Hill, is a home of the small-leaved lime, but seems largely given over to quarrying work above. A walk perhaps for determined naturalists only.

    The best preserved ashwood in the Mendips is at **Rodney Stoke**, a nature reserve, *490 503*.

Weston Woods *310 to 332 626*, ♀, *open woodland*
With all its charms Weston-super-Mare has also a fine wood. Beech is common, though not, I think, native, amongst oak and chestnut, with yew, and the wood is nearly as original looking as those in the Mendips, the sea and sands below adding quietly to its charm. The bramble layer is almost absent, and you can

In Weston Woods: a misshapen beech stem coloured green by algae

two species, and there is lily of the valley.

Blackmore Copse, *928 648*, is a nature reserve of Wiltshire County Naturalists' Trust.

Westonbirt Arboretum *849 897*, ♀ ♣, *160 acres (plus 'reserve' ground)*, *FC*

In Gloucestershire, but almost in Wiltshire, on the A433, 3 miles south-west of Tetbury, is the most comprehensive tree collection in Britain with 5000 species of trees and shrubs. Since 1956 the Forestry Commission has been in charge, but planting has continued systematically since 1829. A centre caters for every reasonable need, rather seasonally. The grounds are open every day until sunset, dogs are allowed, riding is by arrangement. Parking is costly, but you can walk in for nothing. The bus from Cirencester or Bristol stops at the gate.

Maps and guides available are scrappy and nearly useless: the 1968 colour guide booklet is out of print – being revised I hope. As with most Forestry Commission parks, the public is assumed to be not very interested in trees except for autumn colours, brilliant blooms and an occasional 'gee-whizz' tall tree. A large-scale atlas is in the process of compilation but it will be much too cumbersome to be published in portable form. Labelling of the trees is thorough, with one or two gaps and inaccuracies.

Broadly, there are two large woodland units. To your left as you approach is Silk Wood, with mostly younger trees and more open planning than, on your right, beyond the pastureland, the older, very richly planted, Down Plantation. Straight ahead, almost counting as a third unit, and beyond the various offices, is the smaller Down Covert. This is navigated by Circular Drive and is linked to the complex maze of Down Plantation by Loop Walk and Main Drive – all these are signposted. In Down Plantation, Holford Ride, 60 feet wide, is aligned on the house (Westonbirt School, across the main road and out of bounds). Beyond Holford the complexity of species peters out into open woodland of larch and spruce. The road end of Holford Ride is linked to Pool Gate, nearest the car park, by Specimen Avenue, containing

enter anywhere along the mile or so of toll road which begins near the Victoria Pier – from the main promenade road, round the headland.

NEAR CHIPPENHAM

Colerne Park and Monks Wood
837 727, ♀, *111 acres, fp, WT*

Access is from the village of Thickwood, west of the woodlands. This is an important tract of oak and ash (wych elm now dead) in an area not notable for woods. As with many Woodland Trust properties, there is much work to be done. Solomon's seal grows here in

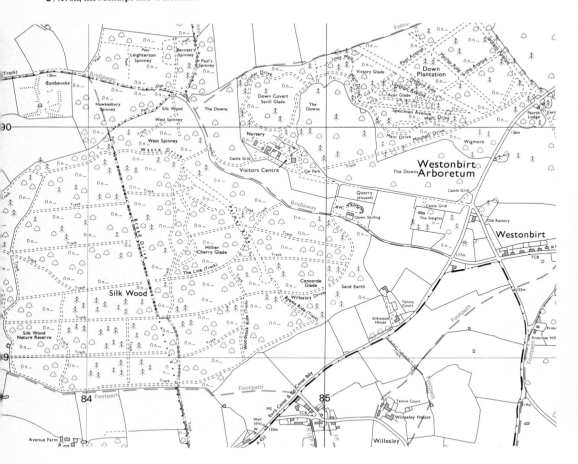

the oldest firs and others. The many paths of the old plantation are lined with large, old conifers of every kind, many so tall that you literally need a telescope to see the foliage. Some have reached so high above the forest that they have been damaged by exposure to the wind. Others are in impressive groups, as the *Sequoiadendron* at the centre of Holford Ride, incense cedars and Brewer's spruce in Maple Glade, redwoods on the Main Drive south of Specimen Avenue, and Lawson and other cypresses, and cedars, on Mitchell Drive – at the edge of the woodland and visible from the approach road. The Down Plantation is rich in maples, *Sorbus* species and horse-chestnut species, and there are many large, old oaks, including the native species and the red oaks as well as planes, particularly a broadly

spreading oriental plane, the impressive Chinese necklace poplar and of course many other broadleaves.

For the widest range of conifers, a comparatively short walk in Silk Wood, along Willesley Drive – the gate is sharp left from the approach road – brings you to Sand Earth (signposted left) and other informal swards richly set out but not yet over mature. Oaks are largely concentrated in the central and western areas of Silk Wood. To walk right round the arboretum part of Silk Wood is a matter of 2 miles, not much perhaps, but a whole day's march if, like me, you pause at every specimen and investigate every small glade and clearing, led on by curiosity and wonder at the variety and majestic forms of these trees, none of which is ordinary.

Part of Silk Wood, Westonbirt Arboretum: a Brewer's spruce

Westonbirt is comprehensive and it is difficult to pick out any single item of interest – you are almost certainly going to be seduced by some exotic beauty on the way to see it. The task of getting to know it all is formidable but richly rewarding. Planted, planned and maintained with loving care over a century and a half, this arboretum is a great deal more than a collection of trees. Trees and shrubs from many scattered and varied habitats combine together to give a unified effect of grandeur yet with many small glades and islands of intimate quality. Nowhere is one conscious of the skills and efforts that have been applied. Each tree, whether it is the giant Nikko fir (north of Loop Walk) or the tiny white-berried *Sorbus discolor* (Whitmoor Bottom, south-east) looks quite happy where it is.

On balance, for a woodland walk, I would recommend the Silk Wood path; it is worth it just for the sudden revelation of the Brewer's spruce, foliage spread like a majestic stage curtain, or for the poetic style of a Japanese larch in a clearing (Concorde Glade). Corsican pines here look quite different from their commercial forestry brothers. There are plenty of larger shrubs as well: for instance you are welcomed by *Cotoneaster* × *watereri* at the parking place, and there are tree hydrangeas, shrub and tree magnolias on the Circular Drive.

Bowood, Calne *970 703*, ♀ ♣, *82 acres, woodland and woodland walks, pf*
This is a mature collection of fine trees, nicely spaced on assiduously mown lawns and no

Trunk of *Pinus ponderosa*, Bowood

obtrusive shrubbery: you won't need your wellingtons here. Bowood does not quite fit our conditions of availability (not open on Mondays, then only afternoons from April to September), but it makes up for this by the extreme thoroughness and clarity of the booklet, which lists every specimen under genera with a key to its position in the grounds, and, vice versa, summarizes each section of the grounds identifying the trees. You really cannot go wrong.

The pinetum is centred on a great western yellow pine, *Pinus ponderosa*, one of several in the country which date from the introduction of the species in 1828. There is an unusually large and sprawling Monterey pine which allows close inspection. Douglas firs, young and old, grow side by side. All in all this is a very accessible introduction to the important conifers. Broadleaves are equally well represented by young and old trees. A great poplar hybrid, 'Robusta', is by the lake and there is a good range of oaks, including the Lucombe oak. An ancient oriental plane and numerous interesting shrubs – including an inky purple hazel – are close to the house. On the formal terrace clipped Irish yews perform a static minuet, watched by an indifferently sculptured half-size nude. Tea is served.

Phillips' Woodland Park *839 525*, ♀ ♠, *80 acres, easy, named paths, pf*

Signposted from the Westbury outskirts, this pleasant working wood also works for visitors, who pay to park or camp but may then roam at will, with tree and bird leaflets to guide them.

A feature of the wood is that the paths are named like streets and identified in a leaflet map so that children can find their own way. There is a tea-room and a museum. It is pleasant to find a private country park.

Cones on *Pinus radiata*, Bowood

Savernake and the Downs

Landranger sheets 173, 174, 184

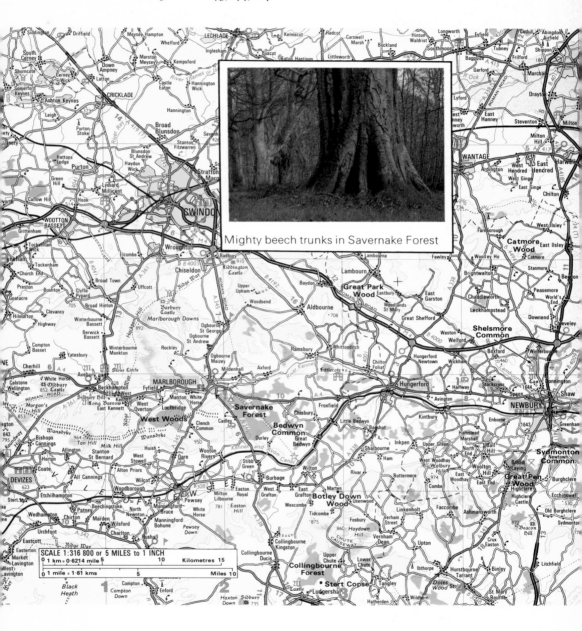

Mighty beech trunks in Savernake Forest

SCALE 1:316 800 or 5 MILES to 1 INCH
0 km 0·6214 mile 5   10   Kilometres 15
0 1 mile · 1·61 kms   5   Miles 10

Savernake Forest *195 682*, ♀, *(♣)*, *28,000 acres, FC*

Savernake (with two short 'a's) means 'Severn oak' – Severn being a common river name. The forest rises steeply from the eastern streets of Marlborough south of the Kennet. Marlborough is a curiously beautiful place, the people well fed and mostly farmers, foresters or teachers. There is still the atmosphere of a coaching town, and even with Woolworths and Waitrose the High Street still has an unbroken line of shops with verandas over the pavement. The journey to London took three days and nights in the seventeenth century, shortened in about 1800 to one day – in the summer. In the early nineteenth century the railway was successfully resisted by the Ailesbury family, whose head is the hereditary warden and owner of the forest, by descent through the Seymours from the Esturmeys, who had it from King John. The railway was never allowed through the forest, so in the years of urban expansion Marlborough stayed small, under the protection of the forest at its side.

In King John's time it was 98 square miles, but this was not allowed in Magna Carta, and land was eventually disafforested to reduce the area to 13 square miles in the reign of Edward I. The bounds of the central bailiwick in about 1300 place the centre near Bedwyn Common. It was not a heavily wooded forest, perhaps more a productive and, usually, well-managed piece of land. For instance, warrens, let in the sixteenth century, had to pay rent of 1520 rabbits to the warden at Tottenham Lodge. Two keepers in the early eighteenth century, based at Braydon Hook and Savernake Lodge, had several underkeepers and earned:

> £10 per annum plus £40 in perquisites; all the firewood they wanted; 14 acres of land; feed for 20 sheep and 20 lambs, 3 cows, 2 horses. They got half the value of all deer skins, dues for deer, profits from bracken; and they imposed a tax for every Marlborough commoner's horse that they branded.

A large part of the forest was enclosed in the seventeenth century, 2200 acres being left unpaled. The forest decayed somewhat. In 1814 the then warden, Charles Brudenell,

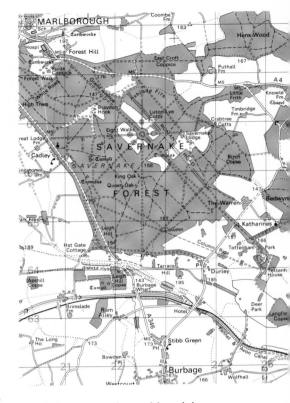

married money and was able to join up scattered coppices in a great planting programme, using oak and chestnut and starting nurseries to stock the forest with 'oak, beech, elm and fir'. Grassy walks were planned, with advice from landscape gardeners. Brudenell's father Thomas had already established the Eight Walks in a star shape typical of early eighteenth-century landscape planning. But Charles also spent £250,000 on the house and gardens at Tottenham: it has never been out of debt since, they say.

Nowadays Savernake is a large, old beech plantation bearing little relation to the ancient forest, except in the many ancient pollard oaks which remain. Both the beeches and the oaks are remarkable specimens and occur in great quantity. This is a forest for today, accessible, large and extremely beautiful. For tomorrow it will be a different story. The beeches are already too old – they are amazingly tall – and

The Grand Avenue, Savernake Forest

West Woods, separate from the old Savernake Forest, border on fields

the many old pollard oaks, superb in decay, are gradually succumbing, many shaded by the massive beeches, others hollow and infirm. Everywhere the progeny of these trees begins to threaten change, and the Forestry Commission, which now manages the forest, is not likely to allow a jungle to develop. The greatest trees are in the area called High Trees; among the intervening thickets of junior trees are picturesque old thorns. The King Oak and the Queen Oak, marked on Ordnance maps,

On Botley Down

Primroses in Collingbourne Forest

are gone. There are good timber oaks in this area. The Grand Avenue is lined with enormous beeches, once very regularly, now beautifully grouped in fantastic perspectives. You can drive down this and other avenues. Deer may cross your path at any point.

There are no leaflets or waymarked walks and rather less than the usual Forestry Commission notices, by order of the owners. The Commission runs a pleasant camping area and a large array of barbecue hearths. The forest is full of cars and people on Sundays, but there is enough room, and you can watch a busy crowd of woodland birds from a car that has been standing an hour or two.

Bedwyn Common, at the old centre of the forest, *260 650*, can also be driven into to a degree. It has been coniferized, but the broad rides are very attractive: birch and sallow.

West Woods, *166 667*, south-west of Marlborough, are owned by the Forestry Commission and can be walked in: a pleasant young plantation.

Collingbourne Forest: Stert Copse
272 515, ♀ copse, 50 acres, easy, fp, pf
Not many people in Ludgershall are interested in woods it seems, but they have a beauty on their doorstep. Not quite on the doorstep: turn down Central Street, east out of the town's tiny middle, for Crawlboys Farm. Ten minutes' struggle in the mud of the bridleway brings you to a corner of the forest, an old wood-bank with weirdly contorted hornbeams. The forest interior here is dull. Continue by the footpath across the field to the gate in the fence of the copse. Here among hazel coppice with oak standards are arrayed in profusion the spring flowers which we look for in English woodland, anemones, primroses and bluebells all together, with strongly formed wood spurge as well. The hazel wands are shiny, the oaks mossy, lichenous and burred: blackthorn and sallow at the edges. Further into the wood the coppice has been cut, leaving the oaks clear and dramatic on a floor spotted with the blue, white and yellow of the flowers: a place to feel happy in. Here, no one could believe that woods should just be left alone.

DOWNLAND WOODS

Botley Down Wood *298 600, ♀, 50 acres, 1 hour, easy, fps*
This lovely little wood looks over downland and, beyond the Wilton windmill, to Savernake Forest. Paths and trackways pass on two sides. At its south corner hazel coppice with oaks gives way to scrub and grass; at the west is a beechwood over ancient mounds and a long barrow. These are protected by a bank with more beech, contorted by wind and use and in extreme contrast with their tall brothers in Savernake below: much spurge laurel here. All around are fine, wide views. The timeless silence was ruined by an Army helicopter, aimless apparently, but thunderous. Strangely enough this deafening apparition only emphasized the perfect quiet of the wood.

Catmore Woods *458 804, ♀, 50 acres, easy fps, pf*
Leave West Ilsley opposite the pub; the road passes Parkwood on your right then turns down to Catmore, which is only a farm and a chapel. Just before you reach these edifices the road turns again and is joined by a bridleway, cart track and footpath. Go up the cart track – you can drive to the top of the hill.

This is a fine and lonely place, up in the sky, the wind blowing through dry grasses and a long line of conifers only adding to its mystery. Take the ride between the oaks and the evergreens, then turn into the wood for a classic hazel coppice with oak standards, bluebells all over the ground. It is picturesque and still looks practical, but it is not without its sinister side – mind you don't step into a trap.

A longer walk could be made northwards, climbing over barbed-wire fences; the only footpath eastwards goes over the hill to East Ilsley under the A34(T) Oxford to Newbury road.

Great Park Wood *345 756, ♀ (♠), easy or very rough, fps*
Turn south out of Eastbury for Woodlands St Mary, or turn there north-east from the pleasant B4000, and you will find yourself at what seems the silent centre of our Emerald Isle. In fact the smooth fields are remarkably emerald and weedless, thanks to assiduous spraying with chemicals. Conversely the wood is neglected, a trackless overgrown wilderness, once a thriving hazel coppice with ash standards, some oak, some beech. Drifts and heaps of *Clematis* cover the margins, which are full of elderberries. The wood divides into north-west and south-east halves; access to the latter is easier. Each half contains a bracken

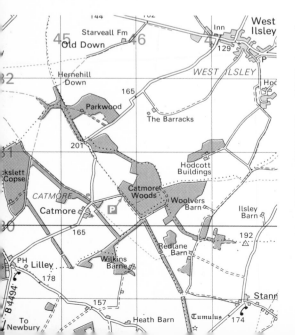

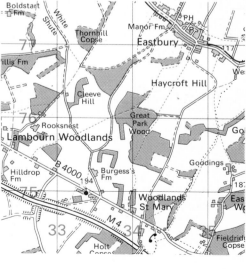

Great Park Wood, with *Clematis*

glade with oaks on a little plateau of less limy soil. There are bluebells and primroses and there would be much more if only this old wood could be taken in hand.

NEWBURY SOUTHWARDS

Over the flat riverside meadows Greenham Common looms dark: again heath vegetation begins, then stops short at a great fence. Fences are illegal on common land, but most of this common was taken over under emergency powers during the last war, as were many others for airfields, now returned to public use. 'Some hundreds of acres' – I quote Newbury District Council – remain as common land. Everyone knows the rest of the story.

Beyond some curiously symbolic burnt gorse and clean new grass stretches **Sydmonton Common** to the south-west. You could walk across it and into the Forestry Commission's plantation, or drive round it to join a road, unnumbered and without fame, which traverses a nearly perfect landscape south towards Watership Down. The Sydmonton Court Estate has many footpaths in and out of the woodland to right or left, and, when you reach the end, a revealing corner.

Here cleaned-up hedges and banks, new-planted cherries, old beech, yew and cherry left to grow, in a tidy, clean, arable environment, are in remarkable contrast to the miserable, dark, overgrown commons and woodland that we see so much of in the south. Beyond, the lines of the Downs enclose a countryside as complex and organized as a good painting, with some massive drifts of *Clematis* left to prove the managers are human. This corner, *489 593*, is worth seeing. It is not a woodland walk but it is a piece of good thinking and decisive action.

Great Pen Wood, *452 622*, is a Forestry Commission parking place and picnic spot hard to recommend, completely surrounded by suburban housing, or on the south side, the forbidding *strictly private* Highclere Park. The wood is gloomy and dank, with a lot of birch and every sort of forestry conifer except fir and Sitka all doing well, and creating a thoroughly funereal environment.

Shelsmore Common *464 709*, ♀, *various easy walks, LA*
This is a popular stopping place with a well-laid-out picnic area including some sheltered tables. Wide birch heath gives way to oak.

SOUTH-WEST ENGLAND
The West Cotswolds and the
Forest of Dean Landranger sheets 149, 150, 162

SCALE 1:316 800 or 5 MILES to 1 INCH

Cirencester Park: Oakley Wood

970 045, ♀ (♣), 1500 acres, 3m or less, easy, muddy, pf

If you are going to walk in woodland it is nice to park in woodland and although it would be feasible to leave your car in Cirencester we suggest the parking place at the map reference. There is some hard surface for winter and wet weather, and some grass (also some rubbish, but, at least, no notices telling you how good the foresters are for preserving the wildlife).

The great beeches here are black and shiny, or clad in moss, or sometimes silver-grey as they are supposed to be. Some are patterned with islands of white lichen. The oaks are black and green on the weather or western side and a lovely pastel grey on the east: ashes likewise. All are fine timber trees and you will find one large area clear-felled – and, as likely as not, logging in progress. Judicious and skilful extraction of the timber leaves a pattern of young trees that can grow to maturity, conifers planted amongst them. This is a working timber woodland with a healthy buzz of activity, as well as deer and plenty of birds.

Towards the south side – Three Mile Bottom – there is a good deal of cherry laurel,

Shapes and colours in Oakley Wood

Beeches in Cirencester Park

which has spread like the weed it is, but it protects the trees, allowing an extra coat of green moss. Some stands are thickly spread with bramble, others on clear ground, for no apparent reason. Everywhere the colours change with a subtle, unrestrained vividness that will be unfamiliar to visitors from eastern England – choose a winter day for this walk. The most 'foresty' bit, with a grassy open ride and a magnificent bank lined with oaks, is at Haines Ash Bottom; it does have ash trees in the bottom. But go as far as you can: the

76

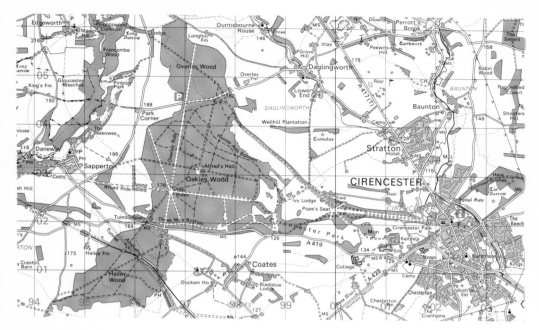

variety of scenery, given that it is nothing but trees, is remarkable, and this wood, Oakley Wood, proves that timber production is compatible with very good landscape – form, colour, texture and composition are all superb. Perhaps I was lucky on a day of racing clouds, patches of creamy sunlight, drifts of brushwood smoke, and a glistening varnish of light rain – but you would not be disappointed on any day.

The road from Daglingworth to Sapperton appears to be a bus route so you could set out from Cirencester and take the bus back. The axis avenue of the park is 4 miles long, east to west. Alexander Pope had a hand in its planning.

Western Cotswold Ridges

The beech is a native tree here and the western folds of the Cotswolds are clothed in some of the finest beech: many woods are open to walkers but the banks are steep and also private residences tend to intervene. Villages like Edgeworth, *947 060*, are impressive, not just charming; and both these adjectives apply to many a corner of the lanes which wander in and out of the escarpments. Again if you explore by car it really is better in winter: less traffic and more to see. Westwards the Golden Valley is of course full of fascinating bits and corners but rarely pure woodland, and with its busy road (A419) and many settlements it is not a countryside for strangers. One piece I have explored around Minchinhampton Common, *855 015*, was fascinating, not least for the trees and bushes in people's front gardens. **Painswick**, *867 097*, has, it is said, 99 yew trees in the churchyard, actually more. This is almost a wood, or two woods since they make two groups, but the yews are clipped to architectural form. Painswick also has its beechwood, with a well-worn footpath climbing into pine towards the Beacon. It is a centre for many walks (set out with great thoroughness in a Gloucestershire County Council booklet, *Walking around Painswick*). **Cranham**, *897 130*, nearer to Cheltenham, has a steep grassy common and beech-covered hill. **Buckholt Wood**, *895 136*, leads by the back road to **Coopers Hill**, *885 138*. Buckholt Wood and Common are Nature Conservancy sites and Coopers Hill has a nature trail from the car park on the main road. I have put them this way round to indicate a preference: the

Coopers Hill car park, with smelly conveniences built of solid, local stone, is on the busy A46 and the nature trail shows signs of being too much tramped around; it is very muddy in winter. The Cotswold Way Path passes through, and so does a pony trail, so that you can hardly see the woods for coloured arrows and notices pointing out fairly interesting things. I eventually found my own route, hopping over a few fences: clearly the Cotswolds edge is worth exploring – and woods of the Cranham area, south-west of Birdlip, are supposed to be the best of our beechwoods; avoid the beaten track, or go the extra mile, to get to know this intimate and intricate escarpment.

THE FOREST OF DEAN

♀ ♠, *285,000 acres, countless walks, many picnic sites, FC (National Forest Park)*
Like the New Forest, Dean was a royal forest before Domesday and remained under the

Crown until taken over by the Forestry Commission in the 1920s. It is a rough, upland plateau of Old Red Sandstone bearing Carboniferous rocks which outcrop variously. Ridges of Mountain Limestone look over the deep Wye Valley to the west.

Between the Severn and the Wye the Dean is on the road to nowhere. It is full of coal and iron and the iron has been mined since Roman times or before. With iron below and deep forests of oaks, with deer, above, it continued a mysterious and self-sufficient existence for many centuries. The people were independent and unruly, the country covered with 'irregular tracks and horrid shade so dark and dreary as to render its inhabitants more fierce and audacious in robberies' – William Camden, 1607. Most of the foresters were miners, and to this day any man born in the Forest of Dean who has worked a year and a day in a mine has the privileges of a Freeminer, entitled to dig for iron ore or coal under licence from the Crown. The King's Gaveller once took a third

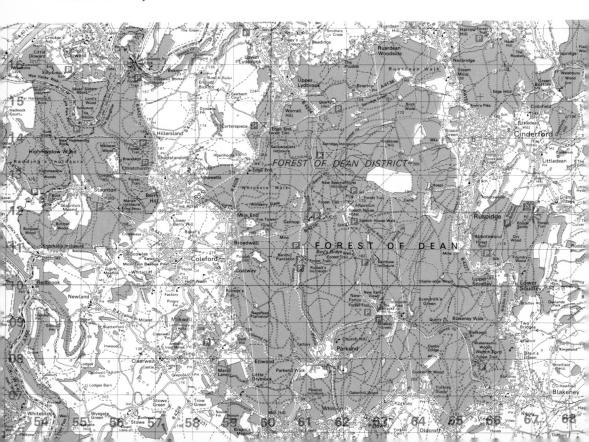

of the profits: now the Deputy Gaveller at Coleford still grants the 'gales', and small two-man drift mines (along the 'drift' of the rocks) are still working for coal, all the major collieries being long since closed.

Between the thirteenth and seventeenth centuries over sixty forges were at work in the forest, some fixed, some itinerant, each using at least one oak tree a week as well as dead and dry wood. Coppices were maintained for charcoal for the fixed forges.

The Dean oaks were needed for the Navy and iron working was effectively stopped at least for a century after 1650. The Commonwealth Government attempted to replant some 16,000 acres: '400 huts belonging to poor people were thrown down. As a result riots broke out . . . fences were broken down, cattle driven into enclosures and wood set on fire' – John Rogers, 1941. This struggle between government and people is a continuing story of the forest. Why did not the Crown take over the mines as it was often advised to do? The answer must be that 'free' is not an empty word. The miners, like commoners elsewhere in England, had rights extending back to 'Tyme out of Minde', as the miners' ancient charter puts it. They were Freeminers before there were any effective kings.

The Miners' Court, where miners took the oath on a stick of holly, was eventually moved to Speech House (620 122, finished in 1680) where also a Verderers' Court attempted to preserve the vert and venison. The court still meets four times a year. The forest was divided into six 'walks', each with a keeper and a lodge – one can be seen at Danby Lodge, 645 083. Other lodges were destroyed by angry miners. Freeminers could sell their gales and 'foreigners' opened large collieries in the nineteenth century such as Trafalgar, New Fancy, Go On and Prosper, Strip and At It: by the 1920s they produced a million tons a year. Rent and royalties of the Dean mines in 1938 were £17,848. The last large pit closed in 1965. New Fancy's waste-top is now a Forestry Commission viewpoint. 24,000 acres are now under productive forestry.

The forest is very beautiful. The bold shapes of the scenery are further broken by quarries and mine workings and the woodlands are not made any the less interesting by the many trackways, from Roman pavements to disused mineral lines, and other signs and remains of human endeavour. The Forestry Commission's conifer plantations are not allowed to intrude, usually, on a foreground of open oak forest or beechwood, where commoners' sheep graze amongst the trees. The rugged topography tends to abrupt changes in soil and vegetation, and provides constantly changing, distant views of tree-clad hills.

The native oak is the durmast, but sessile oaks were planted for Navy timber. Only 200 trees were estimated to remain after one Sir John Winter, with a royal grant in the seventeenth century, removed 30,333 trees.

There are many picnic places arranged along scenic drives and elsewhere and trails intersect at some points. All the waymarked Forestry Commission walks are over 2 miles.

The Scowles 606 046, ♀ ♠, 200 yds, uneven and muddy, private but open

There is no parking place to speak of on the road (B4231, Bream to Lydney), but there is a large lay-by ¼ mile to the south-east. Approached by a lane full of blood-red puddles are the gloomy caves – 'Scowles' – of ancient iron workings: a scene full of the atmosphere of a picturesque grotto with the added interest that it was a place of work. It is now overgrown with tall beeches and shattered yews, full of ferns, but with the dark red rock sculptured by the miners it is a great open wound of the landscape, bones exposed, flesh removed. You can walk south through the beeches to recover from this disturbing experience, but this wood is outside the Forest Park – it leads eventually to Lydney Castle.

Speech House Forest Trail 623 123

The Court Room is now the dining room of the Speech House Hotel (obtain a trail leaflet here) and can be seen by non-diners at 'reasonable hours'. The trail (3 miles long, shorter route of 1¾ miles) includes an old inclosure, coppice chestnut, open oak country on sandstone, a

reclaimed tip as a picnic place and even high-tension power cables. An ancient holly tree is said to have been planted for winter fodder. There is a picnic place amongst old oaks at stop 12. There is also a Spruce Drive planted mostly in 1900, of Norway spruces now tall and well bushed, and a lake made in 1974 for wildlife. It is fed by a brook and is surrounded by damp woodland with ferns and mosses. The arboretum, east of Speech House, with a fine shelter-belt of redwoods (not so tall as to be remote), includes many interesting and attractive firs and really lovely 'exotic' birches, with southern beech and most other specimens you would expect among 200 different species. The lay-out is informal, but the labelling of the trees is scrappy.

Wench Ford Forest Trail *655 080*
Short trail (3 miles) in mature oakwood, schools trail (3 miles) with mine workings, Forest Lodge of Charles II's time, geology notes in leaflets, 'grand old yew', railway sidings grown over and enormous pipe for stream made of old boilers. Longer trail (4 miles) is energetic with spectacular views.

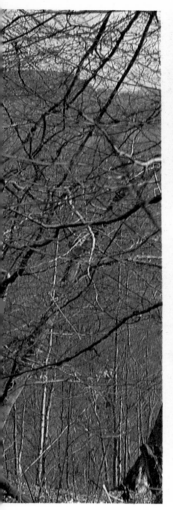

TOP: a Dean miner
ABOVE: The Scowles
LEFT: in the Forest of Dean, near Bream

Blackpool Bridge, $\frac{1}{3}$ mile north of the picnic site, is a former railway bridge over a minor road to Cinderford beside which, a few yards along, can be seen a section of an ancient paved roadway, the Dean Road, possibly Roman.

Edge End Forest Trail *597 142*
The large picnic site is set back from the main road, A4136, but unfortunately you have to cross the road to the trail. The leaflet, good on topography of views, is informative on trees (but not the Weymouth pine stand between stops 2 and 3) and birds, and notes three mine workings abandoned in 1960 but with equipment still in place. The mine is only 200 yards from the picnic site and well worth looking at. Complete trail $3\frac{1}{4}$ miles, shorter route 2 miles.

There are trails also at **New Fancy** viewpoint, *628 096* (parking for coaches), **Abbotswood**, *658 109*, and **The Wilderness**, *659 169*. This last has three loops and is largely concerned with non-woodland features, hot on geology and herbs: it even includes massive waterworks, more pylons, and boggy ground 'once the home of sundew'. The leaflet also includes a reading list.

Symonds Yat Forest Trail *565 160*

Everyone wants to see the rock and there is a
charge for the coach and car park. Leaflet from
a superb log cabin. Viewpoint over Wye.
Durmast oaks of all ages. Very small
arboretum with 'lovely fir', *Abies amabilis*,
trapped by honeysuckle into uncharacteristic
bulges but still lovely. Dive in at the end of the
trail near the road for this and an attractive
young oakwood.

Buck Stone *542 122*

The Buck Stone is at 915 feet with distant
views of the Black Mountains. It can be
reached by a short walk from the end of a lane
out of Staunton. From the post office turn
right then left and fork right on to a dirt road
leading west. After the gate walk 500 yards
then turn left through the older, open
woodland to the rock.

For longer walks, 10 miles or over, see the
Ramblers' Association leaflets. The more
picturesque part of the forest to me is at the
south-west edges near Bream and at the south-
east around Wench Ford. There are other
picnic sites with trails. I will only mention
Boy's Grave: unhappily named, it is too
muddy to be safe for cars in winter.

Mallinsons Veneer Mill at Lydney uses
imported timber, the current demand in the
furniture trade being for *Afrormosia* 'teak' etc,
but there is also a demand for figured yew. All
English yew is more or less figured, and
supplies come from the Dean. The factory
formerly used much local elm; so little valued
was it that large squares of veneer were used
for packing bricks, instead of straw.

LITERATURE

Baty, F. W. (1952) *Forest of Dean*, Hale,
London
Edlin, H.L. (ed) (1963) *Dean Forest and Wye
Valley Forest Park Guide*, HMSO, London.
And many others: put in a 'subject request'.

From the Forest Bookshop, Coleford:
Jones (1981) *Walks in the Wye Valley and the
Forest of Dean*, booklet published by the author.
Marfell, A. (1981) *Forest Miner*, published by
the Forest Bookshop.

From the FC Office:
Leaflets for Forest Trails.
Visitors' Guide and map: refers more to the
Wye Valley, lists addresses etc, but little help
in the forest except that it summarizes the
Forestry Commission trails.

Ramblers' Association leaflets: *Waymarked
Paths, Forest of Dean* and *Waymarked Paths,
Highmeadow Woods*.

An Ordnance Survey Outdoor Leisure Map
(1:25,000) of the Wye Valley and the Forest
of Dean is published in addition to the normal
Landranger series.

THE WYE VALLEY

Highmeadow Woods seems to be the name
used for several woods in a separate but joined
western area of the Forest Park which was not
administered by the Crown until 1817. The
area includes Symonds Yat Rock and a great
bight of the Wye in an 'incised' meander begun
600 feet higher than today. **The Christ-
church Forest Trail**, *567 127*, 3½ miles, is
described by the Forestry Commission as
exceptionally interesting and varied.

There is a ferry at Symonds Yat – Yat
means gate, and the river flows through the Yat
dividing the village into west and east – and a
footbridge at the Forestry Commission's
Biblins Youth Centre from **Lord's Wood** to
Lady Park Wood. Most of the woods in this
section are of native trees.

Little Doward Wood *547 157*, ♣,
*1m (seems like 3), rough, steep, dangerous
in places, partly outside Forest Park*

The rough-and-ready parking place indicated
by the map reference is reached from Great
Doward or the hotel at Little Doward and is
close to King Arthur's Cave, and Lord's Wood
and Doward Woods which are known for wild
flowers. Some of the contents of this and other
caves include extinct mammal bones, now in
Monmouth Museum. Going downhill from the
cave (to the right off The Biblins forest road),
you can turn off right at a great beech root, full
of lumps of native limestone, and pick your
way by a little-used path through an ash and

Rocks and whitebeam at Little Doward

chestnut coppice up into beechwood. Soon you reach a massive limestone wall, which you may as well climb over where you can. Continue steeply upwards by the great, grey trunks of beeches, past their prime, and by bushes of spurge laurel to the limestone ledge above the Wye. Here grows a small-leaved subspecies of the whitebeam *Sorbus latifolia*. The largest tree grows very close to a yew – a curious habit of whitebeams, perhaps very easily explained by birds dropping seeds, but not so easily in view of the yew's heavy shade. One small tree grows up out of the crag itself, sheer above the river, and has mistletoe in it. There is ash and maple, with old hawthorns and ruined old beeches.

An easier way to get here might be from the Doward Hotel, but you might miss, in spring, dog violets, wood sorrel, celandine, cowslips, spurge laurel, wood sage, stinking hellebore and green hellebore.

Follow the forest road towards The Biblins for the Seven Sisters Rocks and Lord's Wood, or continue across the footbridge for Highmeadow proper: this eventually brings you to Staunton, mentioned on page 45 for its Buck Stone.

Tintern, once a wire, iron, brass and tin plate centre, is best known for its Cistercian Abbey, largely thirteenth century, drawn by Turner and Girtin, and having had lines written some miles above it by Wordsworth – under a sycamore, of all trees. The Abbey is generally agreed to be best seen from between trees, being a little gaunt close to. The Forestry Commission has it between redwoods, which does not sound appropriate even if the first trans-Atlantic cable *was* made at Tintern.

The road is lovely but obviously can be extremely congested in the summer time. The several walks from Tintern are easy to find. Another, the **Wynd Cliff and 365 Steps**

Walk, starts from a small Forestry Commission car park, *524 973*, a waymarked nature trail somewhat confused with part of the Gwent County Council Wye Valley Walk. If you find the valley claustrophobic, turn uphill opposite the pub in Tintern and turn left and left again for the Fedw picnic site.

Fedw Woods *505 985*, ♀ ♣, *easy but rocky and ankle-twisting away from the forest road, FC*
The picnic site is high with glimpses of the Monmouth hills but sheltered by conifers and with a nicely crafted children's play area. The walk is easy enough for a semi-retired Yorkshire terrier, who regarded it as *his* territory, and there are nice big Douglas firs, then cleared areas of larch with small oaks, gorse and mossy limestone lumps. There is an impressive pine-clad ridge, with beeches and a very fine view of the wide bowl in the hills of which Fedw is the southern side: opposite is Ravensnest Wood, which also I explored but found uninteresting in spite of some massive Douglas firs with offspring seeded along the

Wild daffodils in Dymock Wood

track side. But park at *504 000* for a dull walk by a loudly babbling stream, up a very gentle incline; good if you have a knotty problem to discuss with a friend.

NORTH OF THE FOREST

Dymock Wood *677 285*, ♀ ♣, *about 1150 acres, 2 walks, easy, FC*
For wild daffodils, oaks, larches, beeches, ferns – especially daffodils – turn off the M50 at junction 3 for Gorsley, then left for Kempley, which also has crowds of nice, small daffodils, particularly in the churchyard. Unfortunately the M50 cuts through the small Dymock Forest, so choose your wood up-wind for less noise. **Hay Wood**, east of the road, is more charming, but nearer the road. **Queen's Wood**, to the west, is of maturing oak with yews under, the trail leading to Douglas firs and to wetland by a stream. It is an old forest but bears little sign of it.

Haugh Wood *593 365*, ♀ ♣, *1000 acres plus, 2 walks, 1m and 2m, easy, NT, FC*
A silent hill with an old wood, once belonging to Hereford Cathedral, now partly coniferized. A good parking and picnic place, this is Hereford's local wood (take the B4224 east from Hereford, then the second left turning in Mordiford) and there are many footpaths and bridleways. Overlooking the Wye, snaking in its wide meadows, is a steep western outlier with footpaths from Fiddler's Green or Cherry Hill, Fownhope. This western arm of Haugh Wood is of oak self-promoted from coppice with large yews: here badgers, deer and rabbits are little disturbed, and there are stinking hellebore, bluebells, spurge laurel and elderberry. This last doesn't sound exciting except that it springs around the edges of the yews where the deer shelter and badgers excavate. I hadn't realized that spurge laurel was such a common plant until I came to the Wye.

At **Eastnor Castle**, *735 369*, near Ledbury, is an arboretum, open seasonally, where Atlas cedars date from 1847. North from here the Malvern Hills are a 40-square-mile Area of Outstanding Natural Beauty.

33	34	35
11	**12**	20
9	10	17

SOUTH-WEST ENGLAND
The Cotswolds
and West of Oxford Landranger sheets 151, 163, 164

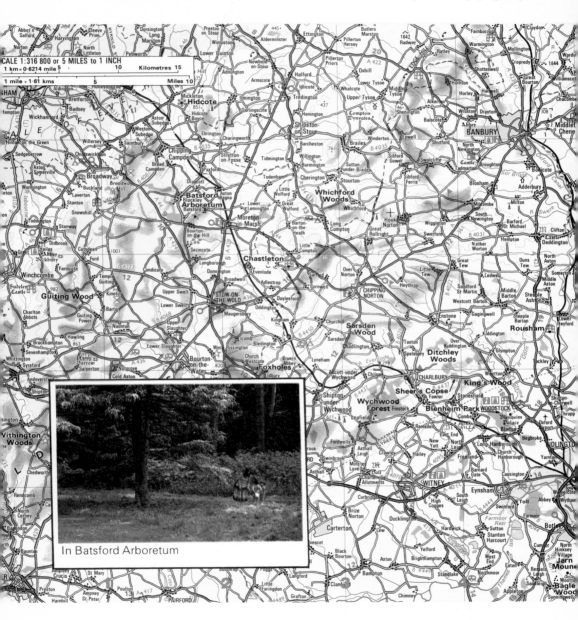

In Batsford Arboretum

NEAR CHELTENHAM

Withington Woods *037 142, rough, 1m or 4m, pf*

High on the Cotswolds is this attractive patch of mixed woodland. Withington village is easily reached from Charlton Kings, the south-eastern suburb of Cheltenham, on the A40 before it takes off into the hills. The road out of the village to Chedworth or Cirencester climbs through the woods, and there are several stopping places for one car at a time. To the left, you plunge at once into the deepening shade of mature larch and spruce, strangely alternating with old oak stubs, many of which have been successfully 'promoted' to produce single stems. With many others, something has gone wrong, and they are dead.

You will soon, if you go quietly, see why. There are more deer than oaks. A vast herd of fallow deer, of all the colours fallow deer can be, lurks in the middle distance, appearing and disappearing in the shadows with the uncanny quietness of their kind. The wood is on very uneven ground and includes ancient earthworks: walking on two feet only is fairly hard.

On the right-hand side of the road from Withington village, facing uphill, is a pedestrian gate leading into a wood which is in fact larger, but with lesser trees; an easier path by small oaks and oldish birches, with some beech. It is perhaps the site of a clearing some fifty years ago. Deer are just as likely here – perhaps a stag with his small harem. When I visited, snow covered the woodland floor, and the paths of the deer were everywhere, joining and parting in the scrub and leading to what mysterious source of food I could not imagine. This woodland continues intermittently for 2 miles to the west, on high ground as far as the escarpment above Colesbourne Park.

The taller woods east of the road are cut by a smaller, little-used road which is probably the boundary of the private Chedworth Woods which surround the Roman villa of Chedworth or Yanworth. This is now occupied by the natives, of course, and heavily exploited under the auspices of the National Trust: not that it isn't extremely interesting, but the woods, hardwood with spruces at regular intervals, are not for walking in.

Guiting Wood *083 258, 450 acres, 1½m easy then 1½m rough, pf*

Woods generally are scarce in the Cotswolds, away from the western ramparts; the land was

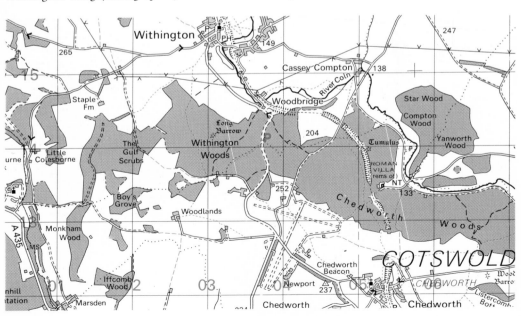

of course mostly used for wool-producing sheep, the profits, or some of them, invested in richly appointed late mediaeval churches like Chipping Campden, Northleach and Burford. Woods remain only near grand houses and tend to be Victorian plantations even when they look wild. Trees there are in plenty, but mostly in the form of shelter-belts, darkly emphasizing and punctuating the wide curves of the hills. Steeper slopes often retain patches of scrub, worth exploring, and there are deep valleys here and there containing tall beeches.

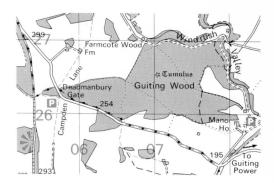

Guiting Power and Temple Guiting, in the valley of the infant Windrush, are richly wooded. Guiting Wood presents two different sorts of woodland walk: very easy along a metalled roadway; fairly rough going on the footpaths in the western half.

Leave Guiting Power going uphill by the smaller, triangular green with its not-very-spreading chestnut: about a mile on, the road sweeps down and is joined by a single track, signposted to Kineton. This small road leads to the Manor, private, and to a parking place, *083 258*, specially provided for walkers. From here you can continue on foot, through a gate, on to a metalled road in the valley bottom, and through the wood – about $1\frac{1}{2}$ miles. It is a great

mixture, with tall larches, poplars and spruces amongst lesser-statured natives including ash, oak, beech and wych elm. The road emerges nowhere in particular, leaving you the choice of returning the way you came, or striking off into the woods. For the latter, go not sharp left but fork left, on a rough, muddy forest road until you reach a junction of paths. The left I have not tried: it should bring you out to the hillside. Right is a footpath open but only just, beside spruce and hemlock plantations to Deadmanbury Gate. Straight on is by an old oak coppice newly planted with hemlock, and

BELOW: Guiting Wood

out to the Winchcombe road; then there is a choice of routes back to the metalled road.

AROUND OXFORD

Beyond the ancient Port Meadow in north Oxford is the tree-covered hill of Wytham, an oakwood. It is not available to the ordinary walker because it is a University mouse-catching, owl-observing and caterpillar-counting preserve. Here a great tit, making 700 visits a day to its nest-box, was persuaded to take 700 self-portraits with 700 different tit-bits in its beak – by T. Royama in 1966. Winter moths, whose larvae descend from the oak branches on threads to pupate below, were studied by spreading sheets beneath the trees. Obviously such experiments are not compatible with woodland walkers. However, a footpath from Wytham to Farmoor skirts the woodlands.

Bagley Wood, *507 022*, quite large, and just south-west of Oxford, is also University property. It is dedicated to commercial forestry and casual visitors are excluded. It is cut by two roads, one the 6-lane A34(T) where drivers get an interesting cross-section, including a hollow filled with very special poplars, and can even stop to look, at many lay-bys. At the gateways, however, pedestrians are severely warned away, perhaps in memory of 'a number of scholars and clerks, who, armed as if for war . . . hunted with dogs and greyhounds, taking deer, hares and rabbits, and threatening the lives of keepers, foresters and parkers'. But this was in 1421. You *can* walk in the woods, if you first apply to the Bursar of St John's College for a permit. The forestry here is all of the first class, and varied too.

Jarn Mound *486 024*, ♀, *a few acres, very easy, private trust*
By the north side of Bagley Wood, at Old Boars Hill, is a bit of 'access countryside' belonging to the Oxford Preservation Trust. The road to Boars Hill climbs up from the Abingdon junction of the Oxford ring road, A34(T). Turn right towards Old Boars Hill.

Here your spanking 30 mph must be reduced to a sedate 25 mph, by order, as you pass the gates of Tall Trees, Rustlings, Pleasant Land, Whiteleaf; or Thickets, Thorns, The Warren and Tanglewood House. Jarn Mound is only the crumbling centrepiece of this land, which consists of a spinney, Jarn Heath, a glade of cherry trees and some meadows: all very easy walking (except for the Mound), very domesticated, yet charming – and very close to the far-from peaceful environs of the Dreaming Spires. In fact, Jarn Mound is one of the few places where you can view the said spires without also viewing half-a-dozen large electricity pylons. 'Arthur John Evans, died 1941, created this viewpoint. . . .' We are grateful. (Sir Arthur also discovered Ancient Crete.)

The Heath, or spinney, resembles a stage set for the last act of a comic opera, people with dogs, instead of actors, appearing and disappearing around small clumps of trees. At one corner is a gate into a meadow, which, a notice informs us, was the 'principal foreground' of the poet Matthew Arnold's vision, in *Thyrsus* and *The Scholar Gypsy*. It is not every field you can say that sort of thing about. The venerable cherry trees form a 'wild garden' through which the very young and the very old can potter, safely.

Blenheim Park *442 168, easy, various walks, pf*
Blenheim Park is at Woodstock, on the A34(T), 8 miles north-west of Oxford. The famous large park (Winston Churchill is buried at

A Blenheim cedar

Bladon, the village on its southern border) is an attractive place to walk, but expensive to park a car within, naturally. You can park easily in Bladon, or fairly easily in Woodstock's High Street, and walk in for a few pence. You can enter for nothing by a kissing gate in Old Woodstock – near a row of picturesque cottages on a raised terrace (but here there really is nowhere to park). The north-west entrance, Ditchley Gate, is on the Charlbury road off the A34 just after Judd's Garage, but this is now less attractive – 2 miles of straight carriage drive, uninteresting since the double avenue of elms is gone.

This is parkland, not woodland, but there are ageing Capability Brown beech clumps and clusters of cedars of quite unusual size and naturalness of disposition. The 'most remarkable' cedar of Lebanon in Britain, according to Mitchell, who literally knows them all, is here. It is 85 feet high by 27 feet girth at 5 feet above the ground, with another 15 feet above that clear of side shoots. It must date from about 1640, when the tree was introduced to Britain, for it is slightly bigger than a known original at Childrey Rectory, near Wantage. This mighty Blenheim cedar is near the cascade. There is a fine group west of

the Grand Bridge – you can't miss the bridge – and a scattered stand of blue Atlantic cedars on the east bank of the lake, towards the Woodstock Gate. Beeches are best seen in the hilly, Old Woodstock corner of the park. Some old oaks survive from the former royal Woodstock Park, it is said, but I have only seen ancient elms, now prostrate or removed.

There are new beech clumps in the spirit of the now superannuated Capability plantings; one, entirely of the variety 'Purpurea', I think he would have disliked. But trees are very well cared for at Blenheim.

Rousham, *478 243*, east of the A423 to Banbury, at Lower Heyford, is a William Kent park or garden, with classical statues and follies. The steep bank of the Cherwell, planted in a picturesque manner, is now almost woodland and a good place to walk for a modest charge payable at the house. The walled kitchen garden, with ancient dovecote and old-fashioned plants, is also well worth seeing.

The Grand Bridge at Blenheim

Larch and wild cherry in Ditchley Woods

Oxford University Arboretum, Nuneham Courtenay *555 987, 45 acres, very easy, pf*

The arboretum is 5 miles south of Oxford on the A423, a Victorian collection of conifers, Japanese maples, etc, to which new trees of special botanical or economic interest have been added. A rare patch of Greensand allows the cultivation of calcifuges. (The alluvial terraces of the Thames are mostly limy.) The plantation is informal and resembles woodland, with peacocks as a change from the usual game.

The arboretum is open only between April and September and is closed on Sundays.

Ditchley Woods *397 214, easy, marginal fp and road, pf*

Still no real woodland for Oxford escapers. But beyond Woodstock is Ditchley Park: turn south-west off the A34(T) at Kiddington. The park is not open to the public and it is heavily coniferized. However, the house is only used for conferences, and the foresters are not much in evidence at the present growing stage. You can park at the point marked on the map, walk to the gate down an avenue of cherries, and then turn left under trees along the perimeter wall. You then reach a single-track unfenced road which follows the eastern boundary of the park woods; if you then go through the gates of Lodge Farm and out to the Woodstock-Charlbury road, you are again amongst woodland. **Sheer's Copse**, *392 193*, is solid conifer, but **King's Wood**, *402 194*, is a middle-aged oak plantation with, of course, native shrubs.

The rides of Ditchley Park's larches,

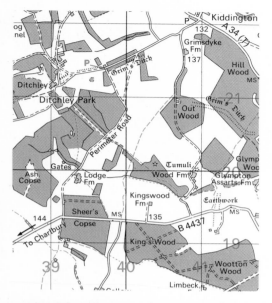

Toothwort and dog's mercury, Ditchley

cautiously explored, will reveal a pair of quite enormous wild cherries, no doubt the parents of several groups hereabouts, and at least four wild service trees. Under the larches are many interlocking rings of fairy-ring fungus, and the grass rides are not without their cowslips and bluebells in season. The straight rides do not resemble old woodland, but the signs of it are there. Along the little road described are beeches and well-formed field maple. Toothwort also grows here, under a patch of old hardwoods – where the foresters stayed their hands. They are to be praised for preserving the cherries and service trees.

Wychwood Forest. The forest is claimed locally to have stretched from Burford to the so-called Oxford Heights east of the city. Domesday Book had it at about 80,000 acres. There are remains of many Roman settlements in the area, villas usually occupying 1000 acres, which with their associated native settlements would suggest that much of the forest was cleared of trees early in its history. By Queen Elizabeth's time Wychwood was a mere 3000 acres somewhere between Woodstock and Burford. Charles I tried to extend it, imposing heavy fines for transgressions of forest law. Throughout the eighteenth century the Oxford gaol held usually three or four Wychwood poachers. There were rights of common only for grazing horses and sheep, and you could be fined for picking up dead wood. An Inclosure Act of 1857 finally destroyed the forest, and the name is now attached to about 1250 acres adjoining Cornbury Park, a hunting lodge of kings past.

Take the Burford road (B4437) out of Charlbury and then the first turning left. This woodland is completely private and devoted to forestry and pheasants, so that we cannot recommend a walk in the woods. Still, the road runs through and around. Residents of Leafield, the ancient village to the south-west, are allowed to collect firewood on Tuesday afternoons. Researchers can get a permit from the Nature Conservancy.

Dotted with old horse-chestnuts and with a dead patch of invading elms, it is not particularly inspiring woodland, even where not coniferized, but there are oddments like a large maple to remind you of the real thing. There is much to be observed in the hedges.

Foxholes *258 208, uneven, CNT*
Wychwood proper is said to survive in a patch of wet birchwood and tangled oak near Bruern Abbey. The wood is partly a nature reserve of the BBONT (Berks, Bucks and Oxon Naturalists' Trust), who has a small parking place at Foxholes Farm: turn off the B4450 between Kingham Station and Bledington to Foscot, then first left on a narrow field lane to Foxholes and through the farm buildings. The map shows the odd shape of the wood at this

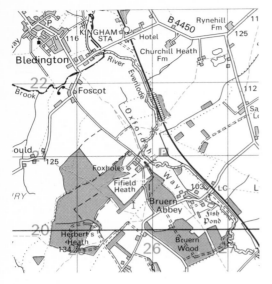

point, but the outline of the southern part is altered by conifer plantations.

Though small as a representation of the great Wychwood Forest, this wood is old, and its varied character carefully preserved. If you want a longer walk than just prowling about the wood, you can strike off to the south-east on a choice of two bridleways with interesting woodland edges and hedges, then out to the road leading to Bruern Abbey, and return along the River Evenlode which, after a short artificial section beside the railway, will lead you wandering back to Foxholes by an easy path: you will have gone 3½ miles. There is an excellent pub at Bledington.

NEAR CHIPPING NORTON

Near Chipping Norton are three short walks: all can be muddy.

Sarsden. Start at the gate, *302 232*, and walk south-west down a newly planted shallow valley, then by the left bank of an ornamental lake. This is a park plantation, with rhododendron and bamboo: nothing special, but nice on a hot day. Keep to the path. You should emerge with Sarsden House on your right; the right of way then continues to the road. Sarsden is a tiny village with good

planted trees, notably *Sorbus* species. You can return by the road past a tumulus planted with beeches.

Whichford Woods. Beyond Long Compton another overgrown plantation occupies an untillable hollow, *295 343*. A bridleway in the bottom and a footpath around the southern perimeter suggest a possible round route – which may be impeded as felling and replanting (with, you guessed, spruce) are in progress. Native trees are oak, ash and beech, but turkey oak and sweet chestnut have been planted in the last century.

A much less wooded walk, at **Chastleton**, leads through an Iron Age settlement to a group of topiary animals in box – *Buxus sempervirens*, which we meet in the wild in the counties around London. The path begins officially at *264 280*, opposite the by-road to Cornwell on the A436, and passes through the centre of the tree-invaded, large prehistoric circular dyke. Ash is the native dominant here. You may then be diverted by a sea of mud to the minor road at the left, along which runs a pleasant open shelter-belt of beech. Continuing north-west you will soon see Chastleton House below; a fine, square block of original Elizabethan design, only faintly resembling a cardboard castle. Here payment of a very small sum entitles you to survey an extraordinary collection of box trees carved into toy animals and chessmen, surrounding a sundial in the somewhat neglected old garden.

Edge Hill, *378 478*, a surprising steep escarpment, is wooded with beech and other trees and can be walked upon. Upton House here looks out to the Midland Plain. Other great houses with gardens nearby, also belonging to the National Trust, make up for the lack of woodland west of Banbury.

Batsford Arboretum *182 332, 50 acres, good paths but steep*
Batsford Arboretum is near Moreton-in-Marsh. Turn off the A44 opposite Sezincote. There is a nice picnic place under tall hybrid poplars, and a garden centre which also sells

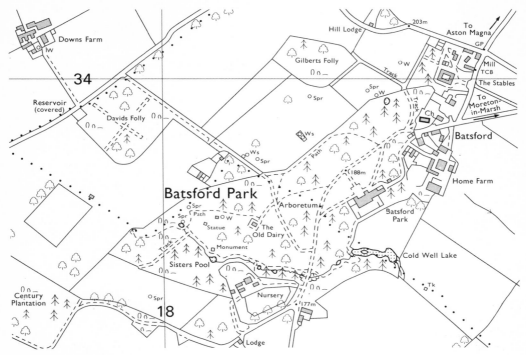

ice-cream and tickets for the arboretum. On this unpromising east-facing hillside is a large and impressively wide collection of exotic trees: some rare, as *Cedrus brevifolia* and Wilson's poplar, or very unusual, as the pendulous form of *Picea omorika* and a blue variety of *Abies nobilis* – this very tall.

Only a small part of the garden round the (rather ugly) house is out of bounds for visitors, who are invited to ramble but offered a suggested walk. This is worth following, and rather than itemize the many beautiful trees we have included a map with some arboreal indications – which cannot be complete. Like all arboreta of any standing, this collection cannot be fully appreciated in one afternoon. It requires several visits at different seasons. Lord Redesdale, who planted this tree garden, was Ambassador to Tokyo in 1850, hence the rather non-U oriental bronzes dotted about. Not all the trees are Japanese; the western American giants are well represented, and as they have been here since about 1860, they really are giants. In spite of the limy soil (Oolite) and the exposure of the site, there are

over forty species and varieties of magnolia at Batsford. The arboretum is officially closed from October to March, but you will not be turned away if you have a definite interest.

Hidcote, *175 430*, 4 miles north-east of Chipping Campden, is a National Trust property with a very beautiful, dramatically arranged garden, notable for its shrubs – some varieties originating here – and with several good specimen trees. There is a hedge-on-stalks of pleached hornbeam beyond a pair of gazebos which are lined with Dutch tiles. There is a katsura and a remarkable cut-leaved elder – even the humble elder has its day – and there are more remarkable specimens listed. A famous avenue of Huntingdon elms, purely decorative and leading nowhere, had to be removed. Hidcote is very popular and rather expensive: worth the money of course, even though on some summer days the scents worn by the female visitors seem stronger than those of the superb roses. As a woodland walk Hidcote is really a non-starter, but impossible to leave out.

Index

Ash, beech and oak are frequently mentioned and therefore are not indexed